The Poems of
Edward Taylor

Recent Titles in
Greenwood Guides to Literature

James Joyce's *Ulysses*: A Reference Guide
Bernard McKenna

John Steinbeck's *The Grapes of Wrath*: A Reference Guide
Barbara A. Heavilin

Gustave Flaubert's *Madame Bovary*: A Reference Guide
Laurence M. Porter and Eugene F. Gray

Ernest Hemingway's *A Farewell to Arms*: A Reference Guide
Linda Wagner-Martin

The Poems of Edward Taylor

A Reference Guide

ROSEMARY FITHIAN GURUSWAMY

Greenwood Guides to Literature

GREENWOOD PRESS
Westport, Connecticut • London

Library of Congress Cataloging-in-Publication Data

Guruswamy, Rosemary Fithian, 1948–
    The poems of Edward Taylor : a reference guide / Rosemary Fithian Guruswamy.
        p. cm.—(Greenwood guides to literature, ISSN 1543–2262)
    Includes bibliographical references and index.
    ISBN 0-313-31781-X (alk. paper)
      1. Taylor, Edward, 1642–1729—Bibliography.   2. Devotional literature,
American—Bibliography.   3. Puritan movements in literature—Bibliography.
4. New England—In literature—Bibliography.   5. Christian poetry, American—
Bibliography.   6. Puritans in literature—Bibliography.   I. Title.   II. Series.
Z8861.4.G87 2003
[PS850.T2]
016.811′1—dc21   2002035330

British Library Cataloguing in Publication Data is available.

Library of Congress Catalog Card Number: 2002035330
ISBN: 0-313-31781-X
ISSN: 1543–2262

First published in 2003

Greenwood Press, 88 Post Road West, Westport, CT 06881
An imprint of Greenwood Publishing Group, Inc.
www.greenwood.com

Printed in the United States of America

∞™

The paper used in this book complies with the
Permanent Paper Standard issued by the National
Information Standards Organization (Z39.48–1984).

10 9 8 7 6 5 4 3 2 1

Copyright Acknowledgment

The author and publisher gratefully acknowledge permission to reprint the following:

Excerpts from *The Poems of Edward Taylor*, Donald E. Stanford. Copyright © 1960,
renewed 1988, University of North Carolina Press. Reproduced with permission.

To Jay, Sara, and Vijay

Contents

Preface

During the last several decades, students and teachers of English studies have gradually realized that the history of American literature did not start in the nineteenth century with the American renaissance. Studies of the literature of colonial America and the early Republic have expanded the canon to include texts from colonial New England, Virginia, and points northward and southward, and lately, the Caribbean and the black Atlantic. Scholars have even begun to explore the possibility of American literature in translation from some of the earliest texts in Spanish, French, and German, expanding our conception of the scope of the literature of early America. The explosion of the literary canon that has had a profound effect on all areas of English studies has focused attention among early Americanists on such esoteric debates as when a work of literature ceases to be British or European and begins to be American, or even when a piece of colonial writing, such as a travel narrative or a sermon, can be classified as a work of literature.

In most undergraduate college classrooms, however, teachers and students still define literary texts as those that can be classified according to traditional genres. The next step, then, to accepting colonial American literature as a legitimate and culturally rich literary period is to isolate the prominent writers of poetry, prose, and drama who were major forces in the development of that period. In the first century of colonial New England, only three poets left behind a large enough collection of poetry to be considered substantial literary figures—Anne Bradstreet, Michael Wigglesworth, and Edward Taylor. Bradstreet and Wigglesworth were major poetic voices in the culture of colonial American Puritanism, published by the religious establishment in hopes of edifying their fellow Puritans as they sought their own salvation. Edward Taylor, however, did not seek publication for any of his poetic output, as far as we know, and yet the discovery of several manuscripts in the middle of the twentieth century has yielded to us the poet who is arguably the chief literary voice of colonial Puritan New England.

This reference is a guide to the poetry of Edward Taylor, establishing why his verse is so significant and central to the study of colonial American literature and the nearly three hundred years of writing that have followed. Since his poetry was discovered in 1936 and a nearly complete volume published in 1960, Taylor's reputation as the premiere early American poet has grown, and his work is widely anthologized and, consequently, taught in most introductory courses in American literature and all courses in early American literature. This book should provide essential background about the New England Puritan culture and the theology in which Taylor was steeped and which had a major influence on the choices he made in constructing his imagery, his prosody, and his overall style. The book also joins other scholarly volumes in the pursuit of a definition of the New England colonial Puritan aesthetic out of which Taylor's literature grew. Although such a definition was never stated in Taylor's time, evidence indicates that he intuited how literature should be written from the Bible and commentaries on biblical texts with which he was familiar.

Because today's students are approximately three hundred years removed in time from Edward Taylor, it is difficult to teach his works in a vacuum. Often the language of his poems and his idiosyncratic spelling are unfamiliar and even obscure to the average student in today's university or college. Overly generalized ideas about Puritans, about their substitution of a belief in the infusion of free grace to replace the vilified Roman Catholic adherence to good behavior as the prerequisite for eternal life in heaven, about the paradoxical nature of the doctrine of predestination, and about the rigors of a God-centered life often tend to gloss over the intricacy of the Puritanism in New England in the seventeenth and early eighteenth centuries and to find it joyless and decidedly unpoetic. This volume attempts to clarify the fine points of what we now refer to as "the old New England way" or "the errand into the wilderness," an intricate amalgamation of religion and government brought by a group of people not able to practice their particular perspective on religion in their own country. They were determined that the way they saw Christianity was not only the sole correct way to be a Christian but also the only legitimate way to entice Christ to come for a second time. The original New England Puritan settlers were people on a mission, deeply feeling a need to establish what their original governor, John Winthrop, referred to as a "city on a hill," open before the eyes of people everywhere and pledged to become the perfect Christian community. Taylor's poetry arises directly out of this concept of reality and human life in which he played a central part.

By the time Edward Taylor reached the shores of the Massachusetts Bay colony in 1668, the mission was almost fifty years old and not nearly as pure as its intentions had been. The first generation of settlers had weathered several heresies, had exiled controversial figures such as Anne Hutchinson and Roger Williams into the wilderness of what is now Rhode Island, and were dealing with the revocation of their charter by the British government. Nevertheless, Taylor sought a solid Puritan education in the ministry at Harvard University and then accepted the pastorate of West-field in the New England wilderness with the objective of forging in that community a settlement that remained as true to the original founders' vision as time and location made possible.

Even as a student in England and New England, Taylor was a versifier, composing occasional poems and required declamations. Apparently to keep himself centered and to shore up his public ministry, however, in 1682 Taylor also began to compose private poetry on a fairly regular basis, perhaps sharing it with friends and relatives, perhaps not, but never seek-ing to publish any of it. Instead, readers of Taylor's poetry surmise that he wrote it to sustain himself emotionally in his pursuit of the Puritan ideal. He had no aesthetic formula and no predecessors to cause the kind of anxiety of influence that Harold Bloom posits grows new poets in the tradition of the old. Yet his poetry reaches beyond the plain style, the term that most literary surveys use to dismiss the structure of the majority of Puritan literary works, and manifests an attentive and playful love of language, imagery, and metaphor that is at once original and also based on his artistic understanding of the language of the Bible.

In the first chapter of this reference I introduce Taylor's work, including the major opus of the *Preparatory Meditations*, which, as he states in its longer title, was intended to assist him mentally and spiritually in the administration of the sacrament of the eucharist, which was part of his duties as Westfield's minister; the long dramatic dialogue poem *Gods De-terminations*; and the minor lyrical and occasional poetry, some of which he collected and carefully transcribed in bound volumes that he left to his descendents, and others that twentieth-century scholars found stuffed inside the binding of the other volumes. A biography of his largely unknown life gives a taste of his wide range of knowledge and dedication to New England Puritan conservatism.

In chapter 2 I analyze the *Preparatory Meditations* as a whole and delve into its meaning as a meditative handbook that charts Taylor's life as the quintessential Puritan who, at the beginning of the volume, has a conversion experience that marks him as one of God's chosen and who, as he proceeds to worship God with that knowledge, is nonetheless beset with the doubts that were meant to keep a good Puritan from becoming too arrogant about his place at God's table. This chapter looks at the structure and meaning of these poems as they reflect traditional Puritan doctrine and also as they manifest Taylor's particular concern with his own talent of writing poetry, which he does not want to waste. It becomes easy for a reader to see, as the meditations proceed, that Taylor equates his own ability to write poetry—which, as everyone's does, varies from day to day—with the state of his own soul, seeing the success of an individual poem as a sign of God's grace and the failure to compose up to his usual standards as the withholding of heavenly favor. In this chapter I also survey several important poems in Taylor's meditative collection, either because they are often anthologized or because they are characteristic of a major theme or movement in his canon. I also analyze *Gods Determinations*, Taylor's valedictory poems, and other occasional and minor poems to show the consistency of Taylor's themes across the entire body of his poetic work.

In chapter 3 I detail the original genesis of Taylor's work and survey what we know about its production, Taylor's revision process, and what happened to the poetry between the time Taylor died and when it was rediscovered in the Yale University Library, the Boston Public Library, and the Redwood Athenaeum. I then survey and evaluate the few editions of Taylor's poetry and the accompanying prose collections that have been published since 1936.

Chapter 4 is an attempt to unveil the complexity of the cultural and historical backdrop against which Taylor composed. The general Puritan mindset that is peculiarly American and, in many ways, significantly different from British Puritanism includes some modifications of the Calvinist doctrines of human depravity, covenant theology, and predestination and election. The need for the settlers on the New England frontier to establish their vision necessitated a community solidarity that made much of their individual pursuit of salvation problematic. Taylor's poetry speaks to this dilemma, as well as to the overriding New Israelite consciousness that strengthened the sense of mission of these settlers in the New World wilderness by creating a spiritual pattern they could follow. A large section of this chapter is devoted to an explanation of the controversy over the opening of the sacrament of the eucharist to the unconverted, a theological storm that had a major impact on the later decades of Taylor's life and on the production of his poetry.

Also in this chapter, I discuss several influences on Taylor's writing. He was able to override the characteristic Puritan distrust of language, particularly literary language, with a reliance on the Bible, also a text, and particularly its poetical books, such as the Psalms and the Song of Songs in the Old Testament. Additionally, his knowledge of the popular analogical system of typology allowed Taylor's poetry to flourish artistically. This chapter is a survey of how this practice, meant essentially to show the entire Bible as anchored in Christ's redemptive sacrifice, provided structure and pattern for Taylor's composition. I also look at the more secular issues of Taylor's classical training at Harvard and the similarity of his work to the British metaphysical poets who were writing in the early modern period and the seventeenth century, establishing the relatively minor degree of their influences on his poetic production.

In chapter 5 I survey several of the ideas, all of them basic to life as a seventeenth-century Puritan, that inform the thought structure and imagery of Taylor's writing. I first discuss Taylor's overriding love for Christ's Incarnation and how its irresistible yoking of the divine and the human provided Taylor, more than anything else did, with the desire to praise God. I then examine the tradition, based in the Song of Songs, of viewing the converted Christian as the antitype of the bride of Solomon in that Old Testament book in her relationship to the bridegroom who is Christ. This allegorical habit explains Taylor's tendency to employ erotic imagery in much of his meditative poetry. I then explore the meditative tradition as a whole and its influence on Taylor. One major misconception regarding the sources from which Taylor drew in the structuring of his poetry is that he was a closet Catholic mystic. I differentiate between Catholic and Protestant meditative techniques to clarify exactly how Taylor perceives the three-part meditative structure that characterizes his meditative poems as well as the nature and biblical imagery that he uses.

In chapter 6 I take an in-depth look at Taylor's major imagery, where it comes from and how he uses it, as well as the prosodic elements that inform the structure of his verse. Taylor's interests mainly in religious ideas, themes, and practices but also in such secular issues as alchemy and the domestic combine to create consciously fashioned and unique poems.

In chapter 7 I survey the reception and criticism of Taylor's poetry from its earliest publication in the late 1930s and early 1940s. Growth in scholarship accompanied a growth in the academy itself and the number of critics who identified themselves as early American scholars. An impetus to know more and more about Puritan New England accompanies the sophistication of the attempts to situate Taylor in his own culture and analyze his poetry from the standpoint of what a seventeenth-century Puritan might want to use as structural principles and imagery.

The book ends with a short bibliographical essay about a few of the major works that have influenced the way modern scholars and teachers consider the poetry of Edward Taylor. Although the number of scholarly books and articles about Taylor's work has diminished in recent years, interest in the classroom continues to grow, and amid all the multicultural flurry of texts of discovery, migration, and settlement, Taylor's poetry continues as a testament to the steady influence of religion in allowing the earliest settlers to overcome the physical hardships of the wilderness with their dedication to the life of the mind and spirit.

1 Introduction

SIGNIFICANCE

Edward Taylor (1642–1729) is one of the earliest poets to emerge from the British colonies of the New World. In his own society and up until 1936, when Thomas H. Johnson noticed a reference to writing by Taylor in a biographical sketch of his life and investigated a manuscript that had lain untouched in the Yale University Library since 1883, Taylor was known primarily as one of the most influential ministers in Puritan New England and as a major participant in the communion controversy that beset the Massachusetts Bay Colony in the late seventeenth and early eighteenth centuries and that, along with the Salem witch trials of 1692, virtually ended the Puritan experiment in the wilderness. From 1939 until the late 1980s, scholars such as Johnson, Donald E. Stanford, and Thomas M. Davis transcribed, edited, and published manuscripts found in the Yale Library and other places containing a large body of poetry, poetic fragments, and biblical paraphrases that Taylor had kept private during his lifetime—some of which he had actually bound inside the self-constructed covers of his finished work. At the same time, other scholars such as Norman S. Grabo and Charles Mignon were editing Taylor's prose work, treatises and sermons, that had also been discovered in various library archives and that appeared to have a connection to and a profound influence on the writing of the poetry. When the magnitude of Taylor's literary output was finally realized, it became apparent that the pre-twentieth-century world had not known about one of the most prolific and talented writers and poets of its earliest colonial days. Ursula Brumm writes that the burial of

Taylor's work in attics and libraries for more than two centuries consti-
tutes "the greatest loss to the development of American literature" (*American* 84).

The rumor has long flourished that Taylor forbade his heirs to publish
his poetry, most likely due to Puritan humility about human endeavor.
By some accounts from his descendents, Taylor even requested that his
poetry be destroyed after his death (Eberwein 63). Charles Hambrick-
Stowe, in his collection of the meditative poetry of Taylor and Anne
Bradstreet, even suggests that some of the scatological and erotic imagery
Taylor uses may have delighted him privately but would have embarrassed
him publicly, so he wished no other eyes to see his work (53). But both
the "Poetical Works," a volume of four hundred quarto pages bound in
leather, and the "Metrical History of Christianity," a long, historically
based poem that also had been ignored for centuries in the Redwood
Library and Athenaeum in Rhode Island, were arranged and bound neatly
enough and apparently revised and clarified by the elderly Taylor as a
complete body of work at some point late in his life to suggest that Taylor
may have harbored a hope that future generations would not be deterred
by this requisite modesty regarding literary production that forced him to
forego publication. Surely the tradition of allegorical scatology and eroticism in biblical exegesis and medieval and early modern Christian aesthetics would have given Taylor the confidence to know that even the
most religious of readers would put this imagery in the proper context.
But Taylor left no will, so proof does not exist for any deathbed intentions. Francis Murphy observes that Taylor also died poor and isolated
enough that his heirs may have never thought to publish his works
(*Diary* 21–22).

John Gatta has suggested an alternate scenario that would fit with the
state of literary transmission from the Elizabethan age through the seventeenth century. A manuscript culture had flourished in England since
early modern times, particularly centered at the court. Such authors as
John Donne and Sir Philip Sidney had participated in this venue for the
dissemination of their writings. Put simply, the manuscripts were circu-
lated among peers, read at private salon readings, and critiqued through
oral gatherings or by letter, particularly at the time that the publication
industry was in its infancy and was looked upon as beneath the attention
of the upper classes. Both Gatta and Jeffrey Hammond suggest that Taylor
may very well have been a popular poet among his peers in New England
in this informal way (Gatta 78–79; Hammond, *Sinful Self* 162–63 and
Fifty 1), although no histories or biographies—even written by his des-

cendents—ever mention that he was more than a minister and a writer of sermons and treatises. We do know that he sent copies of poems to friends in Boston, and several critics speculate, most likely because of the public nature and the subject matter of the poem, that he shared his longer poem *Gods Determinations* with members of his own congregation.[1] Ivy Schweitzer has expressed doubts, however, that he would have shared his meditative poetry in the same way, due to its private nature and Taylor's use of Christ as the intended reader (92). But he still may have asked those who were close to him personally or academically to read and comment on this poetry.

Whichever of these speculations is true, however, the body of poetry by Taylor remains the primary literary testament to the early American poetic strain in Puritan New England and also testifies to his importance in the canon of American literature. Particularly the *Preparatory Meditations before my Approach to the Lords Supper. Chiefly upon the Doctrin preached upon the Day of administration* manifests a familiarity with many of the poetic practices and impulses that dominated poetic production in early modern England, while also reflecting the New England Puritan cultural and religious orientation, and Taylor's own personal encounter with a devotional life in the American wilderness. The *Preparatory Meditations* is notable for its single-minded spiritual quality that precludes much mention of Taylor's actual secular life or physical surroundings. Karl Keller, while agreeing with this view of the poetry, argues that much of Taylor's imagery—that of soldiers, law, finance, medicine, farming, and domestic work—shows a consciousness of what life on the frontier was like in Puritan New England, although Robert Daly observes that he uses such items only metaphorically (Keller, *Example* 55–57; Daly 179). Yet a poet does gather his metaphors from the life and the reading with which he is in contact. Furthermore, Keller finds in Taylor's unpolished poetic form and his use of odd diction and transcription of words a primitive Americanness not totally unlike that of American primitive painters, such as Grandma Moses (*Example* 239–43).

Perhaps a more apt parallel, and a possible source from which Taylor imitated his characteristic roughness, is the *Whole Booke of Psalms Faithfully Translated into English Metre*, popularly known as the *Bay Psalm Book*, published in Boston in 1640 to replace the Ravenscroft edition of the Sternhold–Hopkins psalter that the Massachusetts Bay colonists had brought with them from England. A committee of New England Puritans headed by minister John Cotton found the more liberal translation of the Hebrew by Sternhold and Hopkins to be inappropriate for Puritan worship services. The dogmatically literal translation of the Hebrew they then pledged to accomplish, necessitated by the Puritan belief that words used in worship should not deviate far from those God had sanctioned by placing them in the Bible, makes the Bay psalms often rough and unsingable. Taylor's knowledge and use of this psalter, as well as his belief in the reasoning behind the translation, may be the actual motive for his use of odd phrasings and inverted sentence structure. Still, many early Taylor critics see in his deviations from standard metrical schemes and his idiosyncratic diction and form a tendency to push against convention that is typical of the American spirit.

Despite its twentieth-century discovery, Taylor's poetic canon can be viewed as a foundation for many of the poetic impulses in American poetry written after the seventeenth century: the search for God in nature (although Taylor is beset by a Puritan anxiety about carnality that appears to leave the American psyche after that era), the discovery of one's own identity and place in the world, one's confrontation with the sacred (replicated perhaps less religiously in the twentieth century by poetry of environmental concern), one's use of writing to examine the self, and the manifestation of what later would be called the Emersonian belief—although it is reflected in the writings of the Great Awakening minister Jonathan Edwards as well—that natural life is replete with signs of spiritual truth.[2] In fact, Keller goes so far as to view Taylor as a precursor of transcendentalism through what he terms a certain affectiveness in Taylor's style that leads him to a self-examining vision that he expresses in art. Mason Lowance concurs about the relationship of early Puritan literature to that of the American renaissance, seeing both Taylor and Henry David Thoreau as poets who employ imagery to express their interest in "prophecy and fulfillment" (293–94). Keller also sees this tendency toward the visionary in the writing of Jonathan Edwards, calling it an "antirationalistic" or perhaps more reflective tendency evidenced by the particular sects of American Puritanism that settled in the western part of the New England colonies, which would include both Taylor and Edwards (*Kangaroo* 45–46; Eberwein 62). The length of both the *Preparatory Meditations*, when viewed as a whole, and *Gods Determinations* also seems to some critics to give them the sprawl and even incantatory feel of Walt Whitman's *Leaves of Grass* (Gelpi 32–33). Lowance notes this relationship between Taylor and Whitman, pointing out also the conflation of the personal and the providential that is reflected in Taylor's meditations and also in Whitman's attitude toward the emerging American democracy

(294). Ursula Brumm discusses the relationship between the structure of the biblical analogical habit of typology and the nature symbolism of later nineteenth-century American poetry, particularly of the transcendentalist movement and in the works of Nathaniel Hawthorne and Herman Melville. She also observes a parallel between Taylor and Ralph Waldo Emerson in both the importance of the eucharist to these poets and the way that both of them suffered separation from the mainstream of their religious life due to reactionary or revisionist ideas about the eucharist (*American* 104). Many critics also see a relationship between impulses in Taylor's poetry and that of Emily Dickinson, most notably Karl Keller in his chapter on Taylor and Dickinson in his study of Dickinson, *The Only Kangaroo among the Beauty*. Both Connecticut Valley poets, Taylor and Dickinson were isolated from their mainstream communities, given to a meditative bent, and constantly in search of God's favor (Keller, *Kangaroo* 40–41). Francis Murphy, in his introduction to Taylor's diary, adds Dickinson to the parallel between Taylor and Edwards, citing similar themes and motivations in the poetry of these three prominent Connecticut Valley poets (22). Taylor's unusual vocabulary, his often rough metrics, and his tendency to elide words seem to be a general precursor to the American spirit of independence (Gelpi 31).

William J. Scheick adds that Taylor's "unqualified moral intensity" also sets the tone for much later American literature (161). In this regard, Karl Keller mentions Taylor's inspiration of Joyce Carol Oates, whose book of short stories *Upon the Sweeping Flood* (published in 1966) contains a title story whose plot derives from Taylor's occasional poem of the same name, as well as a poem by Allan Kaplan, published in *Poetry* magazine in 1970, which uses Taylor's imagery and a mention of his name (Keller, *Example* 5). Other later figures of American literature that critics have seen as reflective of the same spirit as Taylor include Robert Frost (for his eschatology), Robert Lowell (for his interest in the remains of New England Puritanism in his book of poetry *The Mills of the Kavanaughs*), and Norman Mailer (whose American dream relates to the errand in the wilderness) (Lowance 294).

Taylor's poetry has also been set to music several times, including settings by Gordon Binherd of "The Ebb and Flow" in 1957 and "Huswifery" in 1958. A composition by Henry Cowell published in 1955 entitled "If He Please" also contains words from Taylor's preface to *Gods Determinations*, and Daniel Pinkham's piece "In Heaven Soaring Up," published in 1985, contains parts of various Taylor poems.

POETIC ACHIEVEMENT

Taylor's poetic achievement comprises a lifetime of work, starting with some early poems composed while he was a schoolboy in London. At Harvard getting his education and later as a minister on the frontier of the Connecticut Valley, he continued to have an active, though private, creative life of many dimensions. After settling in Westfield, he began a twofold existence—as public preacher and community leader and as private poet. Although we may never really know what motivated Taylor to begin writing frequent, consistent meditative poetry, his growing concern for the perpetuation of the Puritan orthodoxy and for more certain knowledge of his own spiritual fate are among the more obvious reasons. Charles Hambrick-Stowe has also speculated that his marriage to his first wife, Elizabeth Fitch, and the subsequent death of some of his young children may have given his life the emotional intensity that resulted in a need for lyrical expression (42).

The *Preparatory Meditations*—Taylor's most well-known because most often anthologized poetry—consists of two series of poems written in a consistent stanza structure of six lines of iambic pentameter with an ababcc rhyme scheme and clustered in recognizable series based on common themes or continual passages from the Bible. According to the dates on the individual poems, Taylor wrote this book over a period of forty-three years. Series One contains 51 poems including those with titles and Series Two contains 167 including those that are numbered separately but are versions of the same poem. Additionally, 89 poems have head-notes from Old Testament books and 129 from New Testament books. Several critics have noted that the majority of the poems have a tripartite structure, not totally unlike that of a typical Puritan meditation or sermon, or a biblical psalm. Critics also see a relationship between the structure and imagery of the *Meditations* and those of the popular early modern emblem books by such writers as Francis Quarles and George Wither, which focus on the iconography of biblical and Christian symbolism as a visual impetus to meditation. Taylor's *Preparatory Meditations* are, by and large however, fairly conventional seventeenth-century meditative or devotional poems written with a stanza structure common to meditative poetry but with Taylor's unique flavor—his unusual and eclectic poetic vocabulary, his ubiquitous promises to use his talents to praise God, his domestic imagery, and his often groveling self-abasement. Most notably, the poems—almost exclusively addressed to the Deity—give the reader an authentic example of the voice of a Puritan saint who has evidence of his salvation and his particular talent as a writer but who still lives in a carnal world beset by the uncertainty that denotes the condition of all of fallen humanity and that places him on an assurance–doubt continuum that gives the energy to these poems and sustains the entire two series.

Because of the complete title Taylor affixed to this book of poetry, most Taylor scholarship takes for granted that each poem (almost all of which are headed by biblical verses) relates to a sermon that Taylor preached to his congregation on a day when he also administered the Lord's Supper, or the eucharist, most likely focused thematically (as the poem is) on the headnote verse. Norman S. Grabo, in both the 1961 and 1988 revised versions of his Twayne book on Taylor, insists that there must be a sermon somewhere connected to every poem, the majority of which are lost or yet to be discovered, and that only studying the two together will allow the reader to understand fully what Taylor is doing (39, 52). William J. Scheick, in one of the earliest critical books on Taylor (*The Will and the Word*, published in 1974), speculates that the sermon-poem connection allowed Taylor to explore similar biblical topics both logically (in prose) and emotionally (in verse) (119). Grabo's publication of two volumes of Taylor's extant sermons in 1962 and 1966, respectively the *Christographia* and the *Treatise Concerning the Lord's Supper*, demonstrated that at the very least, at some points in the writing of the *Preparatory Meditations*, Taylor's mind was focused on the same doctrinal issues while writing both sermons and poems. The most recent discovery of a Taylor sermon collection, *Upon the Types of the Old Testament*, which surfaced in Nebraska in 1977 and was edited and published by Charles W. Mignon in 1989, added evidence to this speculation. All of the thirty-nine sermons in this compilation parallel meditations that Taylor based on typological themes, most notably the first twenty-nine poems of the Second Series. Karen Rowe specifically connects several of the sermons with Taylor's poems on typological subjects, pointing out—in agreement with Scheick—both the similar themes and the dramatic difference in voice between the public, rational preacher of the sermons and the private, emotional praiser of the poetry (Rowe 37, 60, 100–101). Accompanying the evidence of the sermon collections, again based on the title Taylor gave to his book of poetry, is the assumption that he considered writing a lyrical poem a fitting preparation to be able to administer the sacrament to his congregation, a connection of communion and communication with God, which is anchored in Puritan response to the Book of Psalms.

Teachers and critics often deliver the picture to their students and readers of a thoughtful minister sitting down on a regular basis to write a poem to inspire and prepare him to lead his congregation in every eucharistic service (Eberwein 65). Charles Hambrick-Stowe even concludes that, because there are gaps of time between the dating of consecutive poems, Taylor must have gone for long periods without offering communion to his congregation (55), an assumption that accords with the obstinacy that emerges from some of his pastoral decisions recorded in the Westfield church records. Thomas M. Davis, however, in his seminal study *A Reading of Edward Taylor* (1992), indicates that no precise documentation exists that would absolutely link each meditation to any duties Taylor performed regarding communion (14), although the pronounced change in tone that occurs at the beginning of the early Second Series' sequence on typology prompts Davis to speculate that Taylor's increased concern with doctrinal issues connected to the Lord's Supper might have influenced him to become more tied to a pattern that connected sermon doctrine and poem theme sometime toward the end of the First and beginning of the Second Series, a need perhaps for a disciplinary anchor as his relationship to Christ and to the Puritan religion was becoming more volatile (137; Keller, *Example* 76). Davis also connects Taylor's use of the same verse form throughout the 214 poems to such a need, seeing the repetition as a ritualistic form of self-discipline meant to lead Taylor to realize the spiritual promise of every Puritan's life (*Reading* 201–2). Yet despite their repetitive form and whether or not they were meant as mere accompaniments to public sermons, the poems included in the *Preparatory Meditations* are Taylor's most lyrical expression of what he saw as his unique talent for crafting verse. In these poems, he attempts to write himself into being as the typical Puritan—albeit one whose gift was the writing of poetry—while on the Christian walk that is the search for justification, sanctification, and finally glorification.

His long dramatic dialogue poem *Gods Determinations touching his Elect: and The Elects Combat in their Conversion, and Coming up to God in Christ together with the Comfortable Effects thereof* is also contained in Taylor's bound "Poetical Works." Although the manuscript of the poem is undated, Davis places its actual composition between 1679 and 1682, which would position it immediately before or contiguous to the beginning of Taylor's experimentation with meditative poetry. Davis observes that the double concerns in *Gods Determinations* with Native American warfare and the dwindling of Christian church membership could easily reflect Taylor's early attempts to organize his church. During these years, he had to deal with his own reluctant acceptance of the Halfway Covenant of 1662, which had removed baptism as a sacrament available only to the converted and opened it up to unconverted children and grandchildren of church members, thus increasing the number of Christians at Puritan worship services but, in Taylor's eyes, diluting the congregations' purity. Even though the Synod of 1662, convened in Boston by the General Court of Massachusetts, had passed this into law several years before Taylor came to the New World, its repercussions to a minister as orthodox as Taylor were worrisome when he contemplated the possibility that some of the members of his congregation might still be unregenerate. He also had to encourage his congregation to keep faith in the midst of attacks and skirmishes during King Philip's War and after (Davis, *Reading* 27, 64). Hambrick-Stowe also points out that the long poem was composed before Taylor's more lyrical bent appeared following his wife Elizabeth's death (50, 143).

Significantly different for the most part in conception, form, style, and voice from the meditative poetry, *Gods Determinations* consists of 2,107 lines in the form of thirty-five separately titled poems, which are written almost exclusively in iambic pentameter, although a few feature different verse forms. Six of the poems, however, do use the six-line stanza typical of the *Preparatory Meditations*, and Norman S. Grabo has actually termed the long work a kind of Ignatian meditation, which form of devotion also uses dialogue as this poem does (*Taylor* 106–7). All the subpoems in *Gods Determinations* work together to create a dramatic picture of the Last Judgment, with parts of the poem addressing the various groups of Christians that Puritans believed would be present at the event, classified by their status: the Elect who are assured of their salvation, those who are still seeking election and are eager to receive their conversion experiences, those a little more reluctant or indifferent about theirs, and then the whole group together.[3] The poem appears to be removed from Taylor's personal life and, because of that and despite its dialogue, seems to be a significant departure from the meditative lyrics.

The overall work begins with "The Preface" in Taylor's poetic, devotional, but objective narrative voice, which describes the creation of the world and the mightiness of the God who created it. That voice continues in the second poem, entitled "The Effects of Mans Apostacy," which portrays the horror of the apocalypse, particularly as felt by sinful man. The third poem, "A Dialogue between Justice and Mercy," departs from the initial poetic voice and becomes an actual discussion between these two allegorical entities concerning the fate of man and their respective duties toward the regenerate and unregenerate. The remainder of the poems chronicle the final days, with voice given (at various times) to Satan, the soul of man, members of the different ranks of those present at the Last Judgment, and even Christ.

Taylor's body of work also includes a number of occasional poems. He began writing poetry while still a young man in England, some of which he collected in his "Diary, Theological Notes, and Poems" manuscript. The "Poetical Works" manuscript also contains several of Taylor's occasional poems and miscellaneous lyrics, which comprise about three-fourths of his total output (Hammond, "Diffusing" 153). These consist of many short lyrical poems, the most often anthologized or critiqued of which are "Upon a Spider Catching a Fly," "Upon a Wasp Child with Cold," "Upon Wedlock, and Death of Children," "The Ebb and Flow," "A Fig for thee Oh! Death," and "Huswifery." Additionally the manuscript contains a number of elegies and funeral poems written both while Taylor was a student at Harvard and after he moved to Westfield, as well as several love poems to Taylor's first wife, Elizabeth. Several of the poems use acrostics, the abecedarious technique, or emblematic devices in their composition. Additionally, Taylor transcribed three versions of a valedictory poem of several cantos, celebrating his imminent death and entry into heaven. One of his more curious works is "Verses made upon Pope Joan," an attack on the legendary female pope of the ninth century.

Forty-one sheets were also found to reinforce the spine of the "Poetical Works" manuscript, as well as several others in the binding of the *Christographia* manuscript. These contain alternate versions, rough drafts, or copies of some of the *Preparatory Meditations* and other poems and several metrical paraphrases of different biblical books and Old Testament hymns—a poetic exercise that was popular in early modern England and the New World. A "Manuscript Book" also contains drafts and versions of the same poems found in the "Poetical Works."

BIOGRAPHY

Edward Taylor was born about 1642 in Sketchley, Leicestershire, England. No portrait of him exists, and the only physical characteristics reported were that he was a short man with a serious demeanor, as indicated by his grandson Ezra Stiles. He was raised by religious parents and experienced his conversion early, due to the diligent religious instruction of an older sister. In his own public relation of his conversion, Taylor notes that his sister's account of the life, death, and resurrection of Jesus was particularly moving to him at an early age and factored in a large way into his path toward righteousness. He was educated for the dissenting ministry in England, perhaps at Cambridge University, which different sources say he attended for four or seven years. Politically, he believed in the administration of Oliver Cromwell. However, a few years after he left Cambridge, he was dismissed from a teaching position in Bagworth upon his refusal (in accord with thousands of other British clergymen with Puritan sympathies) to take an oath required by the now-restored monarch King Charles II's Anglican-inspired and anti-Puritan Act of Uniformity of 1662. This act also inspired Taylor to write one of his first poems, a mock elegy called "The Lay-mans Lamentation upon the Civill Death of the Late Labour[ers] in the Lords vinyard."

He arrived in Boston on July 5, 1668, after a voyage of seventy days, finding it to be a fairly cosmopolitan town, although not nearly on the scale of London (Murphy, *Diary* 8), and entered Harvard University as an advanced student only three weeks later, after discussions with then-president Charles Chauncey. While a student, he roomed with Samuel Sewall, who would later be a judge at the Salem witch trials, and served as the college butler and, for a short time after he graduated, as scholar of the house. He was chosen as a Class Day orator on his graduation day in 1671 and recited a poem he wrote for the occasion, "My last Declamation in the Colledge Hall May 5, 1671," which praises several languages but finds English to be superior. In his collection of Taylor's minor poetry, Thomas Davis notes that Harvard students were asked to write such declamations every few months. Francis Murphy surmises, and the date and title indicate, that this final one was the graduation speech (Davis and Davis, *Minor* 290; Murphy, *Diary* 9). His intention in attending Harvard appears to have been a desire to become even more appropriately trained as a Puritan minister, seeing the religion as practiced on the shores of the New World as more in tune with the perfect Christianity that all Puritans were seeking. He kept a diary between 1668 and 1671, entitled on its publication *The Diary of Edward Taylor: An Atlantic Voyage: Life at Harvard College and Settlement in Westfield, 1668–1672.* This slim volume describes his migration across the ocean, his college education, and his voyage from Boston to Westfield to begin his ministry.[4]

After his graduation from Harvard in 1671, he was invited to stay on at the university by Chauncey. However, at the same time, Thomas Dewey, a citizen from the frontier town of Westfield, Massachusetts—the settlement furthest west in the New England wilderness—came to Boston to find a minister for their little Puritan community, and Increase Mather recommended Taylor as a recent bright graduate of Harvard. Taylor considered the offer for more than a week and then accompanied Dewey on the hundred-mile trip through the winter wilderness to the frontier settlement. The townspeople found Taylor to be a satisfactory candidate for their congregation, not only as a minister but most likely because he was also a self-taught physician, and offered him fifteen acres of land to move there. They also agreed to build a new meetinghouse to entice him to lead them, but this church was not built and organized until 1679. Until that time, Taylor served Westfield as the unordained and unchurched minister of the town, as well as the town physician and lawyer. The delay in gathering the church may have been occasioned by the effect of King Philip's War on the western Massachusetts colonies, which garrisoned the Westfield settlement from 1675 through 1677, or by the need to gather more inhabitants into the geographical area, although only seven men who had correct knowledge of church doctrine and who were able to relate their conversion experience and offer proof of their election were deemed necessary to gather a church (Koelling 37, Morgan 88–89).

At the official foundation day of the church in 1679, actually comprising two days of festivities, Taylor delivered a sermon, generally referred to as the "Foundation Day Sermon," based on Ephesians 2:22 ("In whom you are also builded (up) together, for an Habitation of God through the Spirit") that employs several metaphors that later become important to Taylor's meditative poetry, such as the conduit pipe, the spicknard from the Book of Canticles, and the allegorical relationship between the wedded couple in the Canticles and Christ and His church. The sermon also begins with an explanation of the dichotomy of humankind reflected in the doctrine of predestination, in terms reminiscent of what Taylor does in *Gods Determinations*. The major image of the sermon, as the biblical verse suggests, is a building, which Taylor uses as a metaphor for the saint and later for the church itself. He pictures Jesus as the cornerstone of the building and the biblical prophets and apostles as the foundation of the saintly house. Taylor used the sermon to voice his reluctant acceptance of the Halfway Covenant and attempted to persuade his flock and others at the festivities from neighboring congregations that this measure should be the last compromise that would depart from the strict intentions of the Massachusetts Bay founding fathers (Davis and Davis, *Church Records* xviii–xix). In this spirit, Taylor uses the theme of a community knit together by Jesus and committed to the bonds of love, the same central image that John Winthrop used previously in his sermon "A Model of Christian Charity," which was delivered either before the original settlers of the Massachusetts Bay colony left England or while they were on shipboard before their arrival on the shores of the New World. Like Winthrop, Taylor makes it clear in this sermon as well as its revision that the Christian charity he envisions extends to committed Puritans only. He also

reiterates the absolute necessity of the public nature of the required confession of faith needed to name a person a full church member and suggests that the perfect time for the public relation is "when he is to be
admitted into Communion" (Taylor, "Foundation" 128). Later in the sermon, Taylor emphasizes the importance of keeping sinners and those who
refuse to prepare for communion out of the church, using the biblical
examples of the man without the wedding garment and the foolish vestal
virgins (Taylor, "Foundation" 147–50).

Taylor was one of seven men in the Westfield congregation who related
publicly the account of his conversion that day, a spiritual testimony that
is recorded in the Westfield church records. Ironically, the Northampton
minister and former Harvard University librarian Solomon Stoddard—
who was quickly becoming Taylor's chief theological adversary in the
Connecticut Valley—assisted Taylor with the protocol for the foundation
of the church under the principles of the Cambridge Platform of 1648
and officially accepted the public relation of his conversion experience
and sealed his ordination, even though Taylor's sermon offered a mild
attack on some of Stoddard's practices at Northampton, although not
actually naming Stoddard. At this time, Stoddard's most notable liberalization was his agreement with the need for a church hierarchy in Boston to unite all Puritan congregations (Grabo, *Taylor* 14), a measure that
contradicted the original intentions of the settlers to have separate congregations in New England with no central structure, although he also
had embraced the Halfway Covenant in a way that did not please Taylor.
Stoddard had actually also begun to consider opening the eucharist to
those halfway members who sought to be converted two years before
Taylor's foundation day,[5] but he had been rebuffed by Increase Mather
and so had not made as strong of a case as he would in the late 1680s and
early 1690s (Taylor, *Treatise* xx). When this happened, Taylor revised and
added approximately fifty more pages to the original "Foundation Day
Sermon" manuscript, and this was discovered by Thomas M. Davis in the
"Extracts" volume collected in the Thomas Prince Collection of material
on the communion controversy and entitled "A Particular Church Is
Gods House."

The late 1680s were very difficult for Taylor, due to the New England
smallpox epidemic of 1689, which spread to the western settlements,
including Westfield. At the same time, church records indicate that his
salary became a matter of dispute in the settlement. Nevertheless, he
remained the only officer of the church until 1692 and throughout his
tenure maintained a higher percentage of his settlement's population as
full church members (Davis and Davis, *Church Records* xxxiv).

His personal life, from all indications, was quite happy, although not immune from the tragedy caused by the rough conditions on the New World frontier. In 1674 he married Elizabeth Fitch of nearby Norwich, Connecticut, who bore him eight children (three of whom lived beyond infancy) during their fifteen years of marriage. She died in 1689, at the age of thirty-nine, and his elegy "A Funerall Poem upon the Death of my ever Endeared, & tender Wife Mrs. Elizabeth Taylor" testifies to her spirituality and his love for her. He married a second wife, Ruth Wyllys, also of Connecticut, in 1692, three years after the first Mrs. Taylor's death. At the time, Taylor was fifty years old and Ruth was about thirty-two. From this union, Taylor fathered six more children during the next fifteen years, all of whom lived to maturity. His youngest son, Eldad, was born in 1708 when Taylor was sixty-six. Ruth Wyllys came from a wealthy local family, and this may have been part of the cause of the congregation's wish to lower his salary (Davis, *Reading* 134–35). Although Taylor has no poem dedicated to Ruth, Thomas Davis surmises that Meditation 1.46, dated the same year he married Ruth and headed by a verse from the Book of Revelations: "Rev. 3.5. The same shall be cloathed in White Raiment," perhaps referring to an actual wedding garment, may be at least an allusion to his happiness about that event. The first four lines indicate a sense of amazement:

> Nay, may I, Lord, believe it? Shall my Skeg
>   Be ray'd in thy White Robes? My thatcht old Cribb
> (Immortal Purss hung on a mortall Peg,)
>   Wilt thou with fair'st array in heaven rig?[6]

Consistent with Taylor's attitude toward the heavenly wedding garment that would fit him for glorification, these lines nonetheless would also indicate the surprise of a second marriage when one was past the conventional middle age of his time (Davis and Davis, *Church Records* xi).

Taylor was a lifelong scholar with a thirst for knowledge, as the evidence of his library and the knowledge of his education reveal. His grandson Ezra Stiles indicated that Taylor studied the classics avidly and knew three languages, as his extant college declamation, a mention in his diary of reading a chapter of the Gospel of John in Greek while on shipboard, and some translations of Origen from the original Greek indicate (Keller, *Example* 16; Murphy, *Diary* 33). The training in Ramist logic he received at Harvard is also reflected in the structure of much of his poetry, particularly in its ubiquitous use of antithesis. The martyred French philosopher Petrus Ramus's adaptation of logic from the traditional classical work of Plato and Aristotle informs much of New England Puritan writing, freeing it from the years of scholasticism that the dissenters associated with the hated Roman Catholics. Through Ramism, the Platonic concept of Idealism was Christianized, and Protestant thinkers were able to transmute the theory of the Ideal, where all ideas exist in perfect form, into a conception of the mind of God. The Ramist system's basic practices of breaking down, classifying, and organizing thought and then arguing via dichotomy, contraries, and contradiction is at the heart of the American Puritan experience, adding a belief in logic and right reason to their devotional allegiance to faith and the mysteries of the Christian religion. Perry Miller explains, citing the works of John Preston, the Puritan master of Emmanuel College at Cambridge during the early seventeenth century, as well as the New England Puritan minister Thomas Hooker, that saving grace did not replace reason but merely acted to elevate that gift, which was not taken from mankind by Adam's fall (Miller and Johnson 1: 39). This legacy of logic that so infused Taylor's culture mitigates any alliance he might feel toward Catholic mysticism in the formation of his personal theology or the structuring of his meditative verse.

We also know that Taylor had a library of approximately 220 volumes, quite a sizable collection for that time and location. These included works by other New England Puritans; books on migration, travel, and discovery; many classical works and patristic exegesis; anti-Catholic tracts; and volumes on medicine and science, many of which were copied in Taylor's own hand (Keller, *Example* 20–22). He also consciously kept manuscript compendia of research and writing on alchemy, metallurgy, and herbalism and was particularly fond of work inspired by the theories of Paracelsus on contemporary medical applications of alchemical theory (Clack 17–18). He also owned a copy of the 1678 posthumous second edition of *The Tenth Muse*, written by his fellow Puritan American poet, Anne Bradstreet. The elegy he wrote for his wife Elizabeth furthermore indicates that he and she were both familiar with the poetry of Michael Wigglesworth as well. Taylor's Bible, long lost, was rediscovered in 1971 in the Westfield Athenaeum's Edwin Smith Historical Museum. Francis Murphy reports in a letter to fellow early Americanist Everett Emerson that the Bible was a 1634 edition of both testaments, printed by Robert Barker in London, bound together with a 1628 copy of the Sternhold-Hopkins metrical psalter, which had been printed at the University of Cambridge. Because of the gap between the publication of these two volumes, Murphy speculates that Taylor himself or someone in his family bound the two together ("Letter" 91).

Taylor remained a conservative as the New England colonies developed, staying faithful to the ideal of the "old New England way" that had actually begun to crumble before he reached the shores of the New World. As *Gods Determinations* indicates, he saw the Halfway Covenant of 1662 as watering down the sacredness of the sacrament of baptism by allowing the children of church members to receive it before they gave the public relation of their conversion experiences—let alone had those experiences that would prove that they were of the Elect that were predestined for heaven. Later, Taylor aggressively countered the theology of Solomon Stoddard because it was attempting to make the remaining sacrament, communion, also available to the unconverted. In many extant prose texts, Taylor insists over and over that the Lord's Supper was certainly not a sacrament meant for those who were not assured that they were of the Elect. During 1693 and 1694, he composed his collection of eight sermons entitled *Treatise Concerning the Lord's Supper*, which offered biblical and doctrinal evidence for the reservation of communion to those already converted. Taylor's collection of fourteen sermons on the attributes of Christ, collected as the *Christographia*, was composed between 1701 and 1703. These sermons are linked to several poems in his *Preparatory Meditations* on the same themes. His third extant sermon series, *Upon the Types of the Old Testament*, contains thirty-six sermons on typological themes, written between 1693 and 1706. Taylor also composed a 500-page manuscript harmony of the Gospels, which he started to work on during the mid-1680s and continued until he became too ill to write. This long attempt, fitting into the contemporary tradition of harmonies, which endeavor to make literal historical sense of the writings of the New Testament, only covers Christ's life up to the end of His first year of ministry.

Taylor's stubborn allegiance to traditional theology made his tenure as Westfield's minister often a turbulent one. The matter was not helped by the stress of such events as the French and Indian Wars and the War of Spanish Succession, which made life a constant danger in western Massachusetts throughout the late seventeenth and early eighteenth centuries due to the activity of the regional Native Americans under their colonial leaders (Davis, *Reading* 171; Grabo, *Taylor* 12). In 1713, he refused to give his congregation the Lord's Supper for a period of four months, until they saw things his way in the matter of conversion before communion (Keller, *Example* 32). In 1717, after he lost an argument that resulted in the building of a new meetinghouse over his objections, he refused to enter the new structure for eighteen months after it was finished (Davis, *Reading*

170). His obstinacy was part of a personality that idealistically longed for the realization of the original New England Puritan's dream, John Winthrop's city on a hill, the establishment of the perfect Christian community that would follow all biblical plans that Christ had established for His kingdom on earth. Taylor also continued to believe in the Puritan ideal of separate, self-ruled congregations—covenants sealed among each individual in that theocratic community, as was celebrated at his own church's gathering—even as the society around him became more united and hierarchical in the relationship of the individual Puritan congregations (Gatta 85).

Taylor was an invalid for the last decade of his life and had to give up most of his ministerial duties. He suffered a serious illness in 1720, as he was in the midst of the last few poems of the Second Series of the *Preparatory Meditations*, but regained enough strength to return to Harvard University to receive an M.A. degree that year (Murphy, *Diary* 9). In 1728, he was replaced by Nehemiah Bull as pastor of the congregation, and he lived long enough to see the Westfield faithful accept Stoddard's view on the nature of the Lord's Supper. Taylor died on June 24, 1729, at the age of eighty-seven.

NOTES

1. Critics who agree on this point include Eberwein 70; Hammond, *Sinful Self* 162–63; Patterson 144; and Gatta 102.

2. Karl Keller discusses at some length how Taylor's poetry anticipates the New Light philosophy of Jonathan Edwards, particularly regarding a belief in the equation of beauty and the will to follow Christ (*Example* 177–78). I find this parallel, however, to be a bit far-fetched when applied to Taylor.

3. Daniel Patterson describes this "structure by status" in some detail (136–38).

4. This diary was published in 1880–81 in the *Proceedings of the Massachusetts Historical Society* (18). Murphy reports that it was subsequently lost for many years and then rediscovered among papers in the Redwood Athenaeum in Newport, Rhode Island. Murphy republished the diary in 1964.

5. Morgan indicates that some ministers may have been offering the eucharist to the unconverted as early as the 1660s (146). Davis and Davis observe that Stoddard did not actually open communion for almost ten years after Taylor's foundation day, however (*Church Records* xix).

6. Davis and Davis, *Church Records* xi. This and all lines quoted from Taylor's *Preparatory Meditations*, *Gods Determinations*, and the occasional poems come from the Stanford edition.

2 Content

THE *PREPARATORY MEDITATIONS*

The two series of *Preparatory Meditations*, although both consist of poems of similar prosody and imagery that is almost exclusively modeled after the language of the Bible and the structure of its Hebrew poetry, are markedly different in tone. Their overall meaning, however, remains consistently focused on Taylor's or the persona's search for evidence of salvation within the context of the Puritan conversion morphology of justification, sanctification, and glorification. A span of perhaps as long as twenty months separates the two series, and Thomas Davis observes that the years of that separation, 1692–93, marked a distinctive change in Taylor's attitude toward his own poetry and the craft of writing devotional verse, which itself is one frequent subject of the spiritual search that is at the crux of his meditative poetry. Davis notes that earlier Meditations—particularly those written between 1682 and 1686—are joyous, inventive, and poetic, while the poems of Series Two, which begins in 1693, tend to be more prosaically tied to the doctrine espoused in their biblical headnotes and ordered by external practices, such as typology, rather than lyrical or spiritual impulses that come from the heart of the poet (Davis, *Reading* 138–39). Even a cursory reading of the poems in sequence reveals this to be true.

All the poems in both series, however, center on conflict, ambivalence, and antithesis, the necessary structure of the basic Puritan struggle between assurance and doubt that is manifested in both the subject matter of the poems and the poetic technique. The theme of ambivalence—

what Jeffrey Hammond calls "the paradigm of the saintly metaself" (*Sinful Self* 146)—is constant throughout the *Preparatory Meditations*. Several critics take the stand that the voice of the poem is modeled by Taylor to be a deliberate persona and that the search is a poetic pose, a verbal representation of the constant struggle expected of all those of the earth-bound Elect before death and glorification. In his early book, *The Example of Edward Taylor*, Karl Keller, for example, makes the case that the poetic voice in the *Meditations* is essentially triumphant, verbally becoming the "Taylor of his desires"; eighteen years later, Jeffrey Hammond theorizes that the *Meditations* is written by an idealized Taylor, or better still, a Taylor who is attempting to adopt the persona of Christ, to see himself, his sin, and his attempts at grasping the reality of grace from Christ's point of view (*Example* 74–75, *Sinful Self* 193, Eberwein 67). Still, the voice does not maintain consistency throughout the two series, even if the essential theme remains the same. There is a noticeable shifting in voice and mood when the *Preparatory Meditations* is read as a whole: the earliest poems are hopeful, the middle poems are doubtful and searching, and the last half of the Second Series contains poems characterized by the voice of a Christian anticipating his glorification with a marked degree of confidence. Additionally, within the context of many of the individual poems, the voice's stance shifts among postures of lamentation, praise, and thanksgiving—the three recognizable attitudes that David assumes toward God in the Book of Psalms.

Assuming that the voice of the poem is indeed the author, whether sincere, idealized, or fictionalized, the reader nevertheless can see Taylor's joy—even in the earlier, more lyrical poems—becoming tempered often by the more negative emotions of doubt and fear. Throughout both series of meditations, Taylor constantly expresses a heartfelt belief in his own unworthiness. Almost every meditative poem ends with a couplet that focuses on feelings of uncertainty, both as a Christian and as a poet. He often articulates a tendency to be pulled away from his Lord by worldly concerns, perplexed that the vision of closeness to Christ that he chronicles early in the First Series in the poem titled "The Experience" does not stay with him; as he writes in another titled poem, "The Reflexion": "So much before, so little now!" And Taylor seems to see his flawed poetry as a written parallel to the naturally sinful state that appears to be causing his disconnection from that vision (Hammond, *Sinful Self* 207–8). This allows negativity to creep into the poetry, a little at first and then more and more as the First Series continues. Hammond says Taylor's real concern is that he can't sustain the passionate intensity of the moment of revelation (*Sinful Self* 184). But his concerns are invariably related to his ability to use language as well.

With increasing frequency throughout the First Series, Taylor ties together his recognition that a poem or two is not up to his usual aesthetic standards and his fear that the writer's block indicates that things are not going well for him spiritually. This is Taylor's particular spin on the characteristic and ubiquitous Puritan antithetical play of assurance and doubt that seems ironic in light of the Calvinist belief in predestination. Such a belief indicates that once a person has been elected by God for heaven, this decision will not be overturned. To ascertain election, it was necessary for the Puritan to perceive a conversion experience, a moment when God ostensibly relayed to the seeker that he or she was saved. However, even though these moments of revelation were required by New England Puritan doctrine to be related publically and judged worthy or unworthy by church elders, the experiences still remained essentially internal events, and the Puritan who experienced apparent assurance of his or her salvation could never be absolutely sure that the vision, the feeling, or the conflation of events recounted in the public relation was authentic. Self-delusion and even the intervention of the devil were always possibilities. Thus, Taylor's fluctuation between overjoyed cognizance of God's presence and despairing fear that God was gone or, worse, never really was with him in the first place, reflects the typical Puritan Christian walk, particularly with its emphasis on needed humility in the face of the spiritual unknown.[1] But when the poems begin to speak about Taylor's attitude toward his own writing and its place in his relationship to his Lord and his own spiritual fate, the poetry becomes intensely personal and purely Taylor. That he necessarily links his writing talent with his spiritual status is made clear, for example, by a poetic slip of the tongue that he deliberately fashions in Meditation 1.31:

> Cleare up my Right, my Lord, in thee, and make
>   Thy Name stand Dorst upon my Soule in print,
> In grace I mean, that so I may partake
>   Of what I lost, in thee, and of thee in't.

Although the anxiety that connects his writing ability with evidence of his salvation can be attributed in part to his study of early modern linguistic theory and faculty psychology, as William J. Scheick speculates (103), it also seems to be a more personal attitude about God's granting of particular talent. As the First Series proceeds, with Taylor sometimes writing personal poems about the state of his own salvation and other times writing more objectively about man's relationship to God, thematically illuminated by the words of the biblical passage that he uses as a headnote, his concern becomes more and more apparent and acute. When he reaches Meditation 17 of the First Series, that poem becomes repetitive and in the third verse, Taylor writes:

> My Phancys in a Maze, my thoughts agast,
>   Words in an Extasy; my Telltale Tongue
> Is tonguetide, and my Lips are padlockt fast
>   To see thy Kingly Glory in to throng.
>   I can, yet cannot tell this Glory just,
>   In Silence bury't, must not, yet I must.

Such a verse shows Taylor's dilemma: because he is a poet, he owes God the praises that are his particular gift. Yet the theme on which he is writing, God's greatness and power, traditionally flummoxes anyone attempting to use limited human language, even figurative language, to express it. Additionally, when he cannot produce poetry that is as well-crafted as usual, he appears to suspect that God is deliberately blocking his skill as a sign that his conversion is not legitimate.

This vicious cycle anchored at the heart of his poetry—a major concern in what Thomas Davis terms the dedication to art sequence of the First Series (*Reading* 84) but one that remains constant at least until he begins to use the Song of Songs as his biblical basis later in the Second Series—increases dramatically after Meditation 1.17 and comes to full force in Meditation 1.23. In Meditation 1.24, he even considers taking vengeance on himself due to his displeasure with his attempts to praise God in poetry. From this poem to the end of the First Series, Taylor continues to express severe doubts about his ability to write poetry, calling his attempts in Meditation 1.24 "smutting leaden lines" and linking them to the questionable state of his soul. Davis indicates that some of the poems at the end of the First Series actually become more aggressive about the sinfulness that Taylor connects to his inability to write good poems, with the imagery of self-deprecation and the prosodical roughness of the lines echoing Taylor's despair (*Reading* 107; Grabo, *Taylor* 88). The first verse of Meditation 1.39 illustrates this combination of theme, language, and prosody:

> My Sin! my Sin, My God, these Cursed Dregs,
>   Green, Yellow, Blew streakt Poyson hellish, ranck,

and

> I cannot kill nor Coop them up: my Curb
>   'S less than a Snaffle in their mouth: my Rains
> They as a twine thrid, snap: by hell they're spurd:
>   And load my Soule with swagging loads of pains.
>   Black Imps, young Divells, snap, bite, drag to bring
>   And pick mee headlong hells dread Whirle Poole in.

The breakdown of rhythm in the second line and the awkward uses of enjambment and sentence inversion in the full verse represented here are a stylistic manifestation of Taylor's fear and horror, or what Francis Murphy has called the chaos in his soul that is echoed by such prosodic roughness (*Diary* 20). And again we have a cycle, this time an ironic one—his fear, goaded on by his doubts about his poetic worth and its reflection of the state of his soul, allows him to control the production of his poetry, and thus the verse actually gets aesthetically better, relieving Taylor's anxiety. What some critics have scorned as Taylor's lack of ability may actually be a controlled prosodic attempt to voice the doubt phase of the Christian walk, or even an authentic pursuit of the truth about his spiritual fate.

The several poems at the end of this series that finish with a plea for a connection to Christ that would be repaid by the best praise that Taylor could write, however, seem to comfort Taylor and lessen the degree of self-deprecating imagery (Davis, *Reading* 68, 125–26). As Taylor develops this theme throughout the Second Series, moreover, he begins to transfer the blame from his own inadequacy to the insufficiency of human language itself to glorify God. As Michael Clark has put it, Taylor eventually sees the state of mortal man's words as a necessarily and permanently dim reflection of the Word (77). By the middle of the Second Series, Taylor often poetically expresses a much calmer belief that the perfect language to praise God is not attainable by anyone on earth, but it awaits him and all saved Christians after death and glorification:

> Under thy Banner Lord, enlist thou mee.
>   Make me to ware thy Colours, SAVING GRACE.
> Them flourish in my Life, and make thou mee
>   To beare thy Standerd and thy Banner trace
>   And so me to thy Palace Glory bring
>   Where I thy Standards Glory ere may sing. (Med. 2.117)

His confidence in his own election also appears in this verse, as markedly in the latter part of the Second Series, the theme of his and his poetry's inadequacy appears to fade away. In Meditation 2.106, he forthrightly asks for "a new set of Words" that will allow him to praise his Lord sufficiently. These new words, he realizes in the poem, are available only "in other Realms." This self-assurance coincides with Taylor's growing reliance on passages from the biblical love poems in the Old Testament Song of Songs or, as Taylor called it, the Book of Canticles. Although he uses imagery from this Old Testament book earlier in his poetic career, such as the banquet and flower imagery of the early meditations in the First Series and even the last few lyrics of *Gods Determinations*, Meditation 2.19 begins this strain of imagery in the Second Series, as it interrupts the previous sequence that uses typology with a poem based on a passage from Canticles, "Can. 1.12. While the King sits at his Table, my Spicknard sends forth the Smell thereof." This Meditation begins directly with Taylor asking Christ to "dub my tongue with a new tier of Words," a positive plea that usually comes at the end, not the beginning, of most of the meditations. He also uses the image of spicknard (an oil used for healing) to form a conceit in the poem, referring to his own spicknard as a potential plant that will bloom and reach its full beauty and potency if Taylor is invited to sit at Christ's banquet table, where the oil's smell will lead to "Spicknardisick" tunes that Taylor will sing.

This use of a Canticles headnote that provides a controlling image for the poem foreshadows what begins in earnest with Meditation 2.115, a sequence of poems based on passages from the Book of Canticles, exploring much of its rich, poetical imagery. In this sequence, which spans Meditations 2.115 through 2.153, Taylor begins to manifest a definite optimism about his own salvation that is more powerful than what comes before. Dating from approximately November 1704, this group of poems was written when Taylor was at the age when most Puritan men had already passed away. In fact, during the last fifteen years of Taylor's life, as he suffered from physical illness and the vagaries of old age, the allegory of the Book of Canticles remained his constant poetic theme (Davis, *Reading* 169). Both Davis and Hammond agree that Taylor deliberately turned to Canticles, with its medieval allegorical nature sanctioned by years of biblical exegesis with which Taylor was intimately familiar, as an escape mechanism from the world that continued to increase its carnality and retreat from the orthodoxy that he so loved. Hammond, in writing about these later Meditations, observes that Taylor's concerns in them are often eschatological, or cognizant of the end of the world. He seems

concerned most of all with the end of his own earthly stay and his translation into heaven. His confidence in his own election comes to its zenith,
however, in the valedictory poems, the imagery of which is largely similar
to the latter Meditations in the Second Series, where he depicts himself
assuredly entering "Christs Palace Hall."[2]

MAJOR MEDITATIVE POEMS

Within the *Preparatory Meditations*, several individual poems stand out
as important, either because they express a major movement in the theme
or because they are often selected and anthologized as representative of
Taylor's style or the Puritan aesthetic.

The first poems that seem more significant than others are the three
that are titled, rather than being numbered and headed by a scriptural
passage. "The Experience" and "The Return" are respectively the fourth
and fifth poems of the First Series, and "The Reflexion" is the seventh.
These poems appear to capture imagistically and emotionally a Puritan
conversion experience. If indeed Taylor experienced his own conversion
as a child, the poems may involve a memory or the representative beginning of a typical Puritan converted life. Because the incident that he
narrates happens while the persona/Taylor[3] is participating in the sacrament of communion, involves a beam of light and flame, and makes the
poem's speaker feel nearer to God than ever before, the account accords
with the typical Puritan moment of assurance of election. "The Experience" is also the first poem in the *Preparatory Meditations* that ends with
Taylor's ubiquitous wish to be able to praise God in the most acceptable
way. "The Return" is an attempt to sustain the vision that inspired Taylor
in the earlier poem and made him believe that he might be one of the
Elect. Its constant refrain, "Oh! that thou wast on Earth below with mee!
/ Or that I was in Heaven above with thee," expresses the poet's longing
as he creates semidoctrinal verses that attempt to gloss the spiritual meaning of the vision captured in "The Experience." Imagery of ladders and
spouts, channels that connect heaven and earth—images that appear in
many of the Meditations—abounds in "The Return." The end of the
poem is extremely positive, with Taylor expressing his realization that he
has had God in his life on earth and thus will be joined to Him someday
in heaven.

Two poems later, however, "The Reflexion" takes a negative turn. Taylor pictures Christ at a banquet, a Canticles-based image for the communion feast that appears more often in the later poems, but he does not

see himself sitting at the table. The earlier image of the spout connecting heaven and earth is depicted as being "stopt [up] / With mud." Halfway through the poem, Taylor tries to convince Christ to return to him by resorting to a poetic explanation of how the fall of man had been followed by Christ's redemptive sacrifice. When a stanza of this objective persua-sion doesn't appear to work, he resorts to reminding Christ of the sub-jective vision that he saw formerly and that he recounted in "The Ex-perience," and ends the poem with a plea that Christ will "Pass o're my Faults" and restore the former sense of assurance.

Thomas Davis notes that these three titled poems may not have been written in a chronological sequence, but they do appear to have been placed in the bound copy of the *Preparatory Meditations* in a deliberate order to reveal Taylor's belief in the nature of Christ's sacrifice and God's subsequent covenant with man, and the related significance of the eu-charist, which would accord with the title of the volume (*Reading* 58–59). But beyond this, the three poems seem to create the reason for being of the rest of the *Meditations*, or what John Gatta calls its "sacred center" (142) as Taylor struggles ambivalently to regain the vision and, later, at least some assurance that he has gone or will go through the pattern of justification, sanctification, and glorification characteristic of the Puri-tan's Christian walk. Jeffrey Hammond observes that "The Reflexion" reveals the sinful self/saintly self dualism that is the focus of his interpre-tation of the entire book of *Meditations* (*Sinful Self* 196), but the three titled poems taken as a whole seem more immediately illustrative of this doubt/assurance theme.

Meditation 1.8 is one of the most frequently anthologized poems in the *Preparatory Meditations*, perhaps because its unity is sharper than many of the other poems, or because its several images are so strikingly original, even humorous, and work together so well. The Meditation has as a headnote "Joh. 6.51. I am the Living Bread," and Taylor uses the image of bread as a conceit, beginning with the surprised persona's discovery of a loaf of bread on his doorstep. This, he tells us, is "the Bread of Life," and in the second verse, it is defined as food sent to replace the "Worlds White Loafe" that had been tasted and then flung away by his predeces-sors, an allusion perhaps to the manna from heaven in the Old Testament. To extend the metaphor further, Taylor creates the astonishing image of God as a baker—a domestic diminishment of the Creator that seems to counter Taylor's later inability to find words grand enough to praise God—and has this holy baker take the ingredients of grace and the "Purest Wheate" that is Christ, knead, and bake a loaf of "Heavens Sugar Cake."

In the context of the poem, not only does the bread of life appear on Taylor's doorstep, but also on his table (where angels have dished it up) and, at the end of the poem, actually in his mouth, where it speaks to him of its presence, creating assurance of salvation.

Two other images, both of which can be related to the emblem book tradition, enrich this poem. The predecessors who "never could attain a morsell more" after they carelessly disposed of their first bread, are pictured not as people, but through the image of a bird of paradise in a wicker cage, a fit emblem for an imprisoned soul in a carnal body. And the images of chutes and conduit pipes, often a feature of Taylor's poems, appear here both as a "Golden Path" that delivers the bread to Taylor's door, and streams of Grace that run from God to man.

Meditation 1.33 is also cited by many critics as an important poem in the Taylor canon, mostly because it is dated July 1789, and is supposed to have been written on the day Taylor's first wife Elizabeth died. One notable feature of the *Preparatory Meditations* is the infrequency with which one sees Taylor's personal life imagistically mirrored in his poems. Some critics have even commented that Taylor might have been writing his poetry back in England as well as in New England, so little do we see of the New England landscape or the personal hardships that Taylor must have encountered on the western Massachusetts frontier in the seventeenth and early eighteenth centuries.[4] Jeffrey Hammond connects this lack of personal detail with what he perceives as Taylor's desire to depict himself as the "timeless" Christian (*Sinful Self* 189), often borne out in the poems by Taylor's attempts to speak objectively about Christian doctrine and man's relationship with God. Indeed, not one of the poems like Meditation 1.33 that are inspired by incidents in Taylor's personal life deal totally with his individual joy or tragedy, but always turn to these universal Christian concerns that are so central to the meaning of his poetry.

The headnote to Meditation 1.33 is "1 Cor. 3.22. Life is youres," which could be a reference to Elizabeth's glorified state after her death, an interpretation that is reinforced by Taylor's reference to envy in the first verse. However, the image of "life" in the poem is also used to refer to Taylor's own spiritual life and the universal life of the Christian. His envy of his wife's newfound closeness to God is balanced in the poem by his chastisement of himself over the more earthbound, mournful feelings he has about her death: "Oh! what strange Charm encrampt my Heart with spite / Making my Love gleame out upon a Toy?" The first two stanzas, as these lines indicate, discuss the familiar Taylor theme of the attraction of carnal relationships that lead him away from his commitment to Christ. But in the third stanza, Taylor cites "Nature," not God or Christ, as finding him to be monstrous for not loving "my [Nature's] life." If the life is Nature's, then that would seem to be the kind of physical life that Taylor's wife has just surrendered or that, perhaps, he himself is thinking of ending due to his sorrow over her loss. Stanza four then, instead of pursuing this line of thought, does a typically Tayloresque thing: it turns to a discussion of doctrine, specifically a comparison of life on earth before and after the fall. Taylor depicts Christ in typological terms, as a "glorious Arke" who disappeared after the fall. But instead of having Christ reappear at the Incarnation, a theme that is otherwise a constant in Taylor's repertoire, he instead wishes for his own soul to be locked up in the ark with the vanished Christ. He declares that, if this happens, his love and his life will again be joined. The different threads in the poem appear to come together here: Taylor actually is comparing the universal Christian grief at the fall of man with his own personal grief over the loss of his wife, and paralleling that with his own search for salvation. His final wish in the poem is to be grafted to the tree of life. Then he could be assured of his own glorification, which would also allow him to live once more close to his wife and to Christ.

Another meditation that is often anthologized, Meditation 2.40, also deals with an actual occasion in Taylor's personal life, this time with more forthrightness than in Meditation 1.33. As in that Meditation and the occasional poem "Upon Wedlock and Death of Children," however, the personal tragedy that forms its theme is still viewed in conjunction with Taylor's own salvation.

Although Meditation 2.40 stands out as the most important poem that relates to Taylor's personal life, actually Meditation 2.36 begins a short sequence that contains 2.40 and that focuses on the necessity of bowing to God's will even in times of suffering. All the poems in this sequence were most likely occasioned by the death of Taylor's twenty-three-year-old son James, which occurred in 1701, while James was on business in Barbados. Meditation 2.40, which speaks specifically to this sorrow in Taylor's life, begins:

> Under thy Rod, my God, thy smarting Rod,
>   That hath off broke my James, that Primrose, Why?
> Is't for my sin? Or Triall? Dost thou nod
>   At me, to teach mee? or mee sanctify?
>   I needed have this hand, that broke off hath
>   This Bud of Civill, and of Sacred Faith.

But as soon as the second verse of the poem begins, we see Taylor focusing not on James's fate, or even his own sorrow, as much as what the untimely death has to say about Taylor's own spiritual state. This would accord with how he pictures his deceased daughters Elizabeth and Abigail in "Upon Wedlock and Death of Children," what Hammond has called "ritual offerings" that serve mainly to illuminate Taylor's spiritual fate ("Diffusing" 173). In the Meditation, he questions God:

> But doth my sickness want such remedies,
>   As Mummy draind out of that Body spun
> Out of my bowells first? Must th'Cure arise
>   Out of the Coffin of a pious son?

He then asks Christ to come to him "out of my James his ashes," not just to comfort him, as would be expected, but also to bring him assurance of his—not James's—salvation. In the last few lines of the third verse until the end of the poem, Taylor then turns to the subject of the poem's headnote—"Col. 1.18. That in all things he might have the Preheminence," and conducts a poetic discussion of Christ's attribute of preeminence, ending the poem with one of his characteristic promises to praise. James is never mentioned again in the poem after the second line of the third verse, even though the poem is seven verses long. Taylor's shift to Christian doctrine may be, as Hammond says, a way to contain his grief ("Diffusing" 177–78), but to the modern reader the poet appears hopelessly self-centered or too obsessive about his own salvation. Aptly, the next Meditation, 2.41, is based on the biblical passage "Hebrews 5.8. He learned by the things which he suffered," but the poem itself is not about Taylor, or the individual Christian, but about man in general. Additionally, the suffering that he undergoes—taking us back thematically to Meditation 1.33—is that of the fall of man.

Meditation 2.80 also assumes importance because its theme is so characteristic of the meditations in the Second Series, particularly in its more joyous, or at least content, consideration of Taylor's usual themes (Davis, *Reading* 176–77). The contrast with Meditation 1.33 emphasizes the relative change in Taylor's attitude as he leaves the First Series and progresses through the Second. At the time he wrote Meditation 2.80, both his physical and spiritual lives were in relatively more stable shape. His second wife, Ruth, was pregnant with his youngest son, Eldad, and Taylor himself was sixty-five years old and approaching his entrance into paradise. Life here is pictured not as locked up in a typological box, but in stanza three, as a series of stairs on which Taylor is walking to heaven. Also, when the poem inevitably turns to the more doctrinal theme of universal man's Christian walk, Taylor now separates himself from and lifts himself above everyman, or as he puts it, "Poor Perblinde man, that squints on things."

But perhaps the most surprising conceit in this poem is Taylor's use of the human act of love and conception of a child to represent metaphorically the process of justification: "The Soule's the Womb, Christ is the Spermodote / And Saving Grace the seed cast thereinto." He also depicts Grace as having to be "brought to bed" before the act of salvation can take place. And his characteristic couplet promising praise at the end of the poem also uses this image cluster: "When of this Life my soule with Child doth spring / The Babe of Life swath'de up in Grace shall sing." The use of such erotic imagery and the metaphor of married conjugal life has roots in the exegetical tradition connected to the Song of Songs, but clearly, the conception and imminent birth of Eldad were also on Taylor's mind as he wrote this joyous poem. Both the spiritual source and the physical event, moreover, are part of the positive emotional mood that the poem expresses.

Meditation 2.130 is also important to the Taylor canon, in that it can be viewed as a representative poem that illustrates Taylor's later conclusion that it is not his writing ability that has problems, but that all human language is suspect when it is used to praise God or to declare His attributes. In this poem, he appears to take in stride the fact that every poet's poetry fails occasionally and that is not necessarily a sign that the writer is not in God's favor. Taylor begins the poem:

> My sweet-sweet Lord who is it, that e're can
> Define thyselfe, or Mine affections strong
> Unto thyselfe with inke? Who is the man
> That ever did, or can these riches Sum?
> Thy Sweetness no description can define
> Nor Pen and Inke can my hearts Love out line.

Not only is Taylor showing the universality of the limits of human language to describe the greatness and glory of God, but he also sees its failure to describe his own feelings toward God. Additionally, his repetition in this verse of the word "sweet" continues throughout the poem, giving poetic illustration to the theme of limited language.

That Taylor has clearly reached a sense of certainty and fulfillment by 1716 when this poem was composed is made clear when, in the fifth verse, he pictures the garden of the Book of Canticles planted with saints, of which he is one. That he returns to the humble stance of earlier Meditations in the next poem, however, indicates that even at this late date he is still poised on the continuum between assurance and doubt. Ensconced as it is in the Canticles sequence, however, this poem renders the assurance much more potent than the doubt.

Taylor's final meditation, 2.165, is based on "Cant. 2.5. I am sick of Love." Although transcribers have not been able to decipher some words in the first verse because of smudging due to Taylor's revisions on the manuscript, the poem clearly returns to the theme of love with which Taylor began the First Series. Hammond sees this poem as a summary of Taylor's poetic life, and surmises that Taylor made a conscious decision to end the *Meditations* with it (*Sinful Self* 234). Clearly it incorporates many of the constant themes of the whole work: the antithesis between the boundlessness of spiritual love and the confinement of mortality, Taylor's conflict between needing to give God his talent of writing and finding that talent to be inferior, and the final promise to sing if God accepts his limited gift. He also uses the emblem-inspired image of the Holy Ghost as a bird who itself presents Taylor with an egg—the gift of saving grace.

GODS DETERMINATIONS

Gods Determinations touching his Elect: and The Elects Combat in their Conversion, and Coming up to God in Christ together with the Comfortable Effects thereof, Taylor's long dramatic dialogue poem, which critic Barbara Lewalski terms a "morality play" (391), is also an important part of Taylor's canon. The characters in the "play" are modeled on allegorical figures popular in seventeenth-century religious tracts that focus on man's search for salvation, and the poem has a distinct tone of didacticism and, as several critics have found, a similar structure to the seventeenth-century sermon (Haims 85, Patterson 136). Jeffrey Hammond distinguishes it from the *Preparatory Meditations* by situating it as a public poem, even though it was never published, a view shared by John Gatta and J. Daniel Patterson, the latter of whom notes as evidence the relative simplicity of the imagery when compared to what Taylor does in the *Preparatory Meditations*. Because the poem is not about Taylor personally, but about his Puritan vision of Judgment Day and the fulfillment of the covenant, it does not have the lyrical intensity of the meditative poetry, although Davis sees similarity between the beginning poems of the *Preparatory Meditations* and the final lyrics of *Gods Determinations* (*Reading* 53). Still, Taylor may have written the poem to work out for himself some of the tenets of his faith (Haims 24). Karl Keller sees all the dimensions of the voice of Taylor reflected in the voices of all the Puritan members of the mythical congregation within the poem (*Example* 131). Davis also sees connections between the imagery in this poem and the composition of the "Foundation Day Sermon," both of which Taylor wrote or began to write in 1679 (*Reading* 28–29).

"The Prologue" that begins the poem is an abstract of its theme and a source of Taylor's theological beliefs (Gatta 108). It starts with a depiction of the creation of the world, with emphasis on God's might in creating a world out of nothing and, more startlingly, being able to end it whenever he pleases: "Whose single Frown will make the Heavens shake / Like as an aspen leafe the Winde makes quake." "The Prologue" ends with a reminder that "Nothing man," or the man who had generously been created out of nothing by this almighty God, "did throw down all by Sin." The poem proper then begins on this note of darkness, turning to the events of the Last Judgment from a focus on man's lack of gratitude for all he has been given, proceeding through the groups of men who are confronting the end of days and chronicling their various fates based on God's judgmental choices regarding their regeneracy. God's wrath is tempered throughout by the words of Mercy and Christ's act of love for God's creation.

In the middle subpoems, beginning with "The Frowardness of the Elect in the Work of Conversion" and "Satans Rage at them in their Conversion" and ending with "An Extasy of Joy let in by this [Christ's] Reply returnd in Admiration," Taylor poetically enacts the paradox of the covenant of grace as it affects those chosen for election. The dialogue among Satan, the elect soul, and Christ reveals that man, due to his legacy of original sin, deserves to be in league with Satan, and Satan knows this. Man in all honesty realizes that he is not worthy of Christ's sacrifice, but in the end, Christ remains merciful and, despite man's acknowledged allegiance to depravity, Christ comforts and saves him from Satan's assurance of his depravity:

> I will you comfort sweet extend.
>   Behold I am a sun and shield
>   And a sharp sword to win the field.
> I'l surely Crown you in the End.

Such carefully written dialogue indicates that Taylor sees as operative in Christian life the continuum of Calvinistic belief between the Old Testament wrathful God and the New Testament loving Christ, as well as the totally free and undeserved infusion of grace that God visits on those He has chosen. Christ puts it thusly in the second "Christs Reply":

> Although thy sins increase their race,
> And though when thou hast sought for Grace,
>   Thou fallst more than before
> If thou by true Repentence Rise,
> And Faith makes me thy Sacrifice,
>   I'l pardon all, though more.

The poem then proceeds to describe the "Second Ranke" and "Third Rank," those who refused to acknowledge the grace of conversion and those steeped in worldliness and sin respectively. These ranks then engage in a dialogue as they try to decide whose fate is worse, and finally turn to the "First Ranke," the saved, to ascertain the limits of mercy.

By the end of the poem, both uncertain ranks realize that they need to depend totally on Christ, and they will then have a chance at salvation. The last six poems are hymns of praise, "Our Insufficiency to Praise God suitably, for his Mercy," "The Soule Seeking Church-Fellowship," "The Soul admiring the Grace of the Church Enters into Church Fellowship," "The Glory of and Grace in the Church set out," "The Souls Admiration hereupon," and "The Joy of Church Fellowship rightly attended." Thomas Davis indicates a belief that the composition of these final verses marks Taylor's maturation as a true meditative poet (*Reading* 45–46). His use of the metaphor of singing for salvation also anticipates much of the imagery in the *Preparatory Meditations*, as well as its distinct modeling on David's songs of praise in the Book of Psalms. And the poem, as a whole, works out the rhetoric of the conversion process, the move from doubt to assurance, that is at the center of all Taylor's poetry.

MINOR AND OCCASIONAL POEMS

Taylor's valedictory poems, meant to bid farewell to his earthly existence, are actually three versions of the same poem, the first two of which Taylor copied into his "Poetical Works" and the third of which he put in his "Manuscript Book." The third version, as the most polished one by modern standards, is generally accepted as the finished version of the poem, even though Taylor included it with other poems that are less polished. All three versions of the valedictory poem were written in the last decade or so of Taylor's life, following his recovery from the serious illness of 1720; their theme of the anticipation of his glorification, as well as their imagistic similarities to later poems in the Second Series of the *Preparatory Meditations*, indicate that he was still an active craftsman even in his later years.

The poem, in all three versions, begins with Taylor bidding goodbye to his earthly possessions, both material and emotional (such as his family). Jeffrey Hammond suggests that the poem actually inverts the creation articulated in the biblical Book of Genesis (*Sinful Self* 230), and it also reverses that Book's attitude, denigrating the nature, despite its creation by God, to which the persona bids goodbye. William J. Scheick suggests that in the *Preparatory Meditations*, Taylor has a positive attitude toward his bodily existence, but that point of view seems to have changed by 1720 when he is ready to bid it farewell (36). His hope in the purification of the Last Judgment, however, causes him to temper his negativity in Canticle 4 of the poem. And the most surprising part of the poem is his unquestionable certainty that he is of the Elect, which appears in most pronounced fashion in the third version of the poem. At the end of Canticle 7 and the beginning of Canticle 8 of that version, he begins to express his characteristic doubts about the reality of his conversion, and then surprisingly admits:

> Faith never holds whats promisd in suspense
> And as I enter do Christs Palace Hall
> He to the Angells Cry, help me to Sing.

The picture here of himself entering the gates of heaven is declarative; Taylor no longer hedges around the possibility, but expresses it as a given.

The poem also contains the most mature expression of Taylor's belief that his problems with language are not the result of personal sin, but merely the state of anything carnal, even words. This theme of the limits of human language and its counterpoise to the anticipated, perfect heavenly language with which Taylor and the other saints will eternally praise God has been with Taylor since the beginning of the *Meditations* (Daly 173), though only thoroughly explored and admitted in the Second Series, but his attitude in the valedictory poems is significantly more optimistic than even in the Canticles-based later meditations.

Several other poems by Taylor found in the "Manuscript Book" are often anthologized. The most popular of these, perhaps because they deal with simple religious themes that are characteristic of the Puritan consciousness, are "Huswifery," "Upon Wedlock and Death of Children," and

"Upon a Spider Catching a Fly." Taylor's use of vivid concrete imagery in these poems has been influenced by the early modern emblem book tradition with which he was familiar and by the habit of Puritan allegory or the analogic view of reality, which allowed a Puritan to see spiritual truth in even the most commonplace natural occurrence (Lewalski 392–93, Eberwein 67). Thus the spider becomes an emblem for Satan who catches hapless humans in his web, and the wasp in "Upon a Wasp Child with Cold" is an analogy for the human soul allowing the warmth of grace to envitalize its parts.

Taylor also wrote elegies for his wife and young daughters as well as for nine public figures. In his extensive work on the New England elegy tradition, Jeffrey Hammond has noted Taylor's use of the elegy to edify the living as well as celebrate the person who has passed on. With his Puritan consciousness firmly focused on the progress of justification, sanctification, and glorification in the individual life, Taylor's elegies highlight the divide between those still living in the carnal, sinful world and those who are being eulogized, often envied by the living (Hammond, "Diffusing" 161, 164). Still, the perception of the community as a group of visible saints allowed the elegies to offer hope that only time—not sin or death itself—separated each man from the fate of the eulogized ("Diffusing" 171). Thus, these elegies focus more on the deceased's path in life and contain the same tone of joy as the later *Meditations*. Hammond also emphasizes their communal nature, calling them "texts of belonging" ("Diffusing" 182).

Taylor also turned his poetic talent to several more mundane exercises that were typical forms of written Protestant devotion. One of his legacies is the unfinished "Metrical History of Christianity," extant at 20,000 lines—the longest poem written in America in its first 150 years—that attempts to characterize the chain of earthly events that, in hindsight, shows the agency of God in human concerns in the western world. The mechanical nature of this poem and its paraphrased derivation from its religio-historical sources, such as Matthias Flacius's *Magdeburg Centuries* and John Foxe's *Actes and Monuments*, show little personal investment, except for a heartfelt virulent attack on Roman Catholicism, and a much different poetic voice from that of the meditative poetry (Davis, *Reading* 139; Keller, *Example* 143, 159). Nevertheless, Taylor's preoccupation with natural wonders, as evidenced by the selections found in his library, the careful notes in his medical compendiums, and some of his occasional poems, such as "The Great Bones Dug Up at Clavarack," emerges in this long poem (Keller, *Example* 154–55). The accounts start with Christian persecutions in 35 A.D. and continue into the Reformation. Taylor ended this project, however, about 100 years before his own century (Davis, *Reading* 174). He finishes with verses about Protestant martyrs in England, and Keller speculates that—had he continued—he would have added the New England experiment and its leaders to the compendium (*Example* 158). Donald Stanford, who published a microform edition of the "Metrical History" in 1962, giving the title to this untitled manuscript, states that he doubts anyone "in his right mind" would want to tackle a complete edition of the poem (Stanford 8). Eberwein has called it the "most distasteful" of all Taylor's poetry (64).

NOTES

1. Karl Keller tries to demonstrate, however, that the self-deprecation Taylor uses is an act (Keller, "Taylor" 192–93).

2. References to Taylor's valedictory poems are from Davis and Davis, *Minor*.

3. I will refer to the persona of Taylor's poems (with the exception of *Gods Determinations*) as Taylor, for purposes of the smoothness of my prose.

4. Davis, however, makes the case that Taylor's poetry takes on particular intensity and becomes more awkward and ambiguous whenever personal situations in his life preoccupy his attention, such as the death of Elizabeth (*Reading* 114).

3   Texts

GENESIS OF WORK

It is clear from the physical evidence existing of Taylor's poetic output that he was a conscious poet who recognized and treasured his own talent as a distinct gift from God. Thomas Davis especially has explored the way Taylor's original texts are presented, the extent of his revisions, and organization of the various poems into books and collections. Although Davis, as other critics, questions whether Taylor composed the meditative poetry at the regular intervals that would tie them to preached sermons or administrations of the eucharist, Davis nonetheless sees Taylor's explicit attempts to arrange the poetry as a reflection of his conscious desire to be a poet and to be accepted by an audience—perhaps his future descendents, perhaps only God (*Reading* 52).

We have evidence that, in 1691, Taylor stopped composing after he wrote the first forty poems of the First Series, reordered and revised those, probably based on the way he saw the scriptural headnotes fitting together (Davis, *Reading* 27–30, 48). He apparently continued to do so every so often, after a number of poems had been written, up to the end of Series Two in 1725. Because of this practice, it remains unclear whether the dates attached to various poems reflect their first composition or the date they were finally revised or even ordered into the book itself, making it even more problematic to ascertain whether or not there is a poem-sermon connection (Davis, *Reading* 50).

Despite speculation about a manuscript culture in New England, we have no certain evidence that Taylor was well-known or lauded by his own community as a poet. Only a few fragments of his verse were printed during his lifetime. The last two stanzas of his occasional poem "Upon Wedlock and Death of Children" were added to the end of a sermon pamphlet of 56 pages written by Cotton Mather, "Right Thoughts in Sad Hours," printing a homily originally delivered by Mather in Charlestown to soothe the parents of a child who had just died. It was published in London in 1689. The verses that actually appear only in the first edition of this sermon, which was reprinted two more times in the nineteenth century, are slightly different from those Taylor placed in his "Poetical Works" manuscript. Thomas Johnson speculates that Taylor did not actually give the poem to Mather, because the two verses also appear at the end of some extracts from a letter Taylor wrote to Samuel Sewall in August 1686, which is also added to the end of the sermon (140). There appears to be a relationship in the production of this pamphlet between Mather and Sewall, with the latter possibly having financed the original publication of the manuscript, which is dedicated to him by Mather (139). Sewall himself had lost three children between 1678 and 1686, which may have prompted Taylor to write the letter and send the verses to his close friend and former college roommate. Additionally, Taylor's elegy for David Dewey, a deacon of the Westfield congregation, was also published in a 1713 pamphlet commemorating Dewey's death. Although Taylor is chronicled in several histories of the Puritan era or the region of Westfield, almost always he is remembered as the founding minister of the Westfield Congregational Church. Only Joseph L. Sibley, who wrote an 1881 biography of famous Harvard University graduates, notes that Taylor also wrote "Sacramental Meditations" and "God's Determinations" (Keller, *Example* 15; Murphy, *Diary* 11). This is, of course, what gave Thomas H. Johnson the impetus to investigate the "Poetical Works" that had lain dormant in the Yale University Library archives for over fifty years.

DISCOVERY

The "Poetical Works" manuscript, Taylor's carefully organized, leather-bound book of 400 pages, had been passed down through several generations of Taylor descendents before his great-grandson, Henry W. Taylor, gave it to the Yale University Library in 1883, along with several other materials associated with Edward Taylor, including the manuscript of the *Christographia* sermons. Taylor's "Manuscript Book" was also presented to the Yale University Library by Henry T. Terry, another descendent of

Taylor, in 1921. Consisting of 54 pages, including 18 that are blank, it contains rough drafts and versions of occasional and minor poems.

Another group of Taylor manuscripts, his "Diary, Theological Notes, and Poems," also passed down through generations of his descendents, was deposited at the Redwood Athenaeum in Newport, Rhode Island, by Taylor's great-great-great-grandson Roderick Terry in 1951. The major work of poetry in that collection is Taylor's "Metrical History of Christianity," bound by him in 1710 and containing 438 pages, 4 of which are blank. Also contained in the same group of manuscripts are Taylor's diary, bound together with a number of his minor poems and poems by others, some notes on theology apparently composed in England, and a folio manuscript of his partial "Harmony of the Gospels" accompanied by the signature of Taylor's grandson, Ezra Stiles.

Additional manuscripts of both early versions of poems found in the "Poetical Works," and exercises, such as psalm paraphrases, were found when the bindings of some of Taylor's own books were investigated. Verse paraphrases of the Book of Psalms and the Book of Job and some of the earliest poems that Taylor wrote in England, as well as many of the occasional poems and elegies, had been used to reinforce the binding in Taylor's manuscript books and the bound *Christographia* sermons, suggesting that Taylor truly considered these to be unpublishable exercises.

The most recent discovery of a Taylor manuscript was made in 1977 in Lincoln, Nebraska. A small quarto of 905 folio sheets bound with material made from Taylor's typical discarded manuscript pages was discovered and Charles Mignon established that the handwriting indicated it was authored by Edward Taylor. It turned out to be a collection of thirty-six sermons on typological themes that accord with the first thirty Meditations and a few later ones contained in Series Two, all of which are also written on typological themes. Mignon edited and presented this work as a two-volume collection from the University of Nebraska Press, *Upon the Types of the Old Testament*, in 1989.

EDITIONS OF TAYLOR'S POETRY AND RELATED PUBLICATIONS

After he located the "Poetical Works" manuscript in 1936, Thomas Johnson subsequently published several of the meditations, some poems from *Gods Determinations*, and three of Taylor's occasional poems in the *New England Quarterly* in 1937, a number of the elegies and a few other occasional poems in *Publications of the Colonial Society of Massachusetts* in

1943, and three other occasional poems and several more meditations in the *New England Quarterly* in 1943. Some of Johnson's selections from Taylor were also included in the 1938 edition of *The Oxford Anthology of American Literature*. Finally, Johnson's first book-length edition of selections, entitled *The Poetical Works of Edward Taylor*, was published by Rockland Editions in 1939 and reissued by Princeton University Press in 1943.

Taylor's addition to the canon of American literature became increasingly certain throughout the 1950s and early 1960s because of Johnson's edition, as well as the anthologizing of certain Taylor poems in such collections as *Major American Writers*, edited by Howard Mumford Jones (1952), *The American Puritans: Their Prose and Poetry*, edited by Perry Miller (1956), and also Miller's *Majors Writers of American Literature* (1962). At the same time, more and more courses in early American literature began to feature his poetry as professors and students started to realize that American literature actually commenced some time before the American renaissance and the fiction of Nathaniel Hawthorne and Edgar Allan Poe.

The "Diary, Theological Notes, and Poems" compilation was located in 1957 by Donald Stanford, who—as mentioned previously—transcribed and published the "Metrical History of Christianity" as *A Transcript of Edward Taylor's Metrical History of Christianity* in 1962 in a microform edition. He also published a number of Taylor's poems from this manuscript in *American Literature* and other journals.

The 1943 edition of Taylor's poetry edited by Johnson had presented, however, only a scattering of the poet's total discovered output, foregrounding *Gods Determinations* as Taylor's major opus. Jeffrey Hammond attributes Johnson's selection of poems to his formalist orientation, which attracted him to the more conventional, straightforward, and unified poems among those he had discovered (*Fifty* 6). Taylor scholarship as a distinct subdiscipline of early American literature actually did not start in earnest until the publication of Donald Stanford's edition of *The Poems of Edward Taylor* by Yale University Press in 1960. Stanford adapted his 1953 doctoral dissertation, a complete edition of all Taylor poems then known and coherent in manuscript form, to the requisites of the Yale publishers, so that the 1960 printed edition included *Gods Determinations* but focused mainly on the meditative poetry. Stanford transcribed over 240 of Taylor's poems and included the entire *Preparatory Meditations* in his volume. He published the collection with a foreword by the noted critic of seventeenth-century meditative poetry Louis L. Martz and with an introduction and appendices that give much information about Taylor, the manuscripts, and Stanford's editorial practices. He also corrected many of the errors in Johnson's original edition, including at Martz's suggestion the movement of "The Prologue" to the beginning of the *Preparatory Meditations* from the beginning of *Gods Determinations*, where Johnson had put it despite the fact that a preface already exists there (Stanford 8). An abridged edition of the poems with a revised introduction by Stanford was published in 1963 by Yale University Press and reissued in 1989 by the University of North Carolina Press, where it is still in print.

In the 1960s, Norman S. Grabo also edited and published two collections of Taylor's prose sermons that have been shown to have distinct connections to the poetry, the *Christographia*, and the *Treatise Concerning the Lord's Supper*. The manuscript of the Christographia sermons was included in the material deposited in the Yale University Library, and Grabo received permission from Donald Stanford to edit the sermons from a microfilm and record-print negative provided by Yale University from their rare-book collection (Hammond, *Fifty* 22; Grabo, "Editing" 13). As Grabo states in his introduction to Taylor's *Treatise*, the latter manuscript was bound with other material in a document entitled "Extracts, by Reverend Edward Taylor, Westfield," written in a nineteenth-century hand (liii). This was collected with the other writings surrounding the Taylor–Stoddard communion controversy and deposited in the Thomas Prince collection at the Boston Public Library. Additionally, Grabo wrote the first biographical and critical study of Taylor, the Twayne *Edward Taylor*, published in 1961 and again in a revised edition in 1988.

Another intensive editing work of several years came to fruition in 1981 with the publication of the series *The Unpublished Writings of Edward Taylor*, edited by Thomas M. and Virginia L. Davis and published in several volumes by Twayne. The Davises had been working since the 1970s on transcriptions of the church records of Taylor's congregation during the period of his ministry, as well as several related sermons including the revised "Foundation Day Sermon," that had been found in the "Extracts" manuscript and that Taylor had enlarged and reworked from the sermon he delivered at the founding of his church. Later, the Davises also transcribed additional Taylor writings from the Prince collection that deal with the Taylor–Stoddard communion controversy as well as Taylor's "Commonplace Book," deposited in the archives of the Massachusetts Historical Society. The final multivolume Twayne publication included three volumes of both prose and poetry—*Edward Taylor's "Church Records" and Related Sermons*, *Edward Taylor and Solomon Stod-*

dard: *The Nature of the Lord's Supper,* and *Edward Taylor's Minor Poetry.* This work was completed by a four-volume transcription of *Edward Taylor's Harmony of the Gospels.*

Of primary interest to this study is the volume on Taylor's minor poetry, which contains several of the poems Taylor wrote while still in England; five elegies and a declamation that he penned at Harvard; many of the occasional poems, elegies, and paraphrases written in Westfield that were published elsewhere previously and some that were not; and some fragments, paraphrases of biblical hymns, and Latin translations that are included in the volume's appendix. The publication of this Twayne volume meant that by 1981, all of Taylor's readable extant verse was in published form. That some of the later American and early American anthologies from the 1990s include parts of Taylor's psalm paraphrases along with selections from the more traditional poetry indicates the growth in attention to Taylor's use of the Bible as a source for his imagery and prosody.

In 1988, Charles E. Hambrick-Stowe published *Early New England Meditative Poetry* from the Paulist Press. This volume includes a small selection of poems from both Taylor and Anne Bradstreet, as well as an extensive introduction about the uses of meditative poetry in New England.

Taylor studies will benefit from the winter 2002 publication of a new critical edition of the *Preparatory Meditations* and *Gods Determinations,* edited by J. Daniel Patterson, and available from Kent State University Press.

4 Contexts

HISTORICAL AND CULTURAL INFLUENCES

Edward Taylor was a typical New England Puritan whose orientation remained extremely conservative even as the second and third generations of Puritan settlers adjusted to the New World and, in many ways, relaxed their original orthodoxy. Just as the earliest New England Puritans combined their social, political, and religious beliefs into a closely knit theocracy, so did Taylor subsume his various interests and curiosities— ministerial, medical, occult, linguistic—into a distinct religious orientation that never leaves the poetic consciousness that emerges from his verse.

General Puritan Zeitgeist

The tenets of the general Puritan spiritual experience—the Calvinistic belief in man's ultimate depravity because of Adam's original sin and the subsequent undeserved and totally free experience of God's saving grace granted through the sacrifice of Christ, the mystery of election in which God chose before birth who was saved and who was damned, and the saints' perseverance on earth where doubt remained the state of the elect soul and prideful assurance of one's salvation would be most likely construed as evidence of delusion and damnation—all surface in a reading of Taylor's poetry (Morgan 70, Lewalski 390, Scheick xii). *Gods Determinations* pictures the Last Judgment in the authentic Calvinistic terms that betray the legalistic mindset of Puritanism. In the third subpoem, "A Dialogue between Justice and Mercy," for example, the figure of Justice adamantly insists on man experiencing the result of his original sin, whereas the figure of Mercy agrees to become "incarnate like a slave" in order to remedy his "Clients Case." Justice continues to condemn those who think they can effect salvation through their own endeavors, but finally agrees to spare those who put their trust in Mercy, figured forth by Taylor as Christ. In the subpoem that soon follows entitled "Gods Selecting Love in the Decree," Taylor depicts "All mankinde [split] in a Dicotomy": the saved ride to the heavenly feast of the Lord's Supper while the "rest" stay behind. Several subsequent subpoems illustrate the weakness of those who are saved coupled with doubtfulness that even Christ's redemptive act could lead to their individual salvations, but "Christs Reply" assures the Elect that He will conquer sin, which is imaged in the poems as a dog who needs to be muzzled and chained. Christ assures the doubtful sinners:

> And though thou do too frequently
> Offend as heretofore hereby
>   I'l not severly blaim.

Thus, the poem shows Taylor's belief in man's incontrovertible depravity and the power of Christ's sacrifice to intervene for undeserving man's salvation. The *Preparatory Meditations*, true to its lyrical format, presents the same vision of essential sin and irresistible grace from the perspective of an individual Puritan soul.

The Puritans' infatuation with legalism in their theology of the relationship between God and man is evidenced most acutely by the covenantal underpinning of this theology, which promulgated the view of God's agreement to reward His Son's sacrifice for the sake of humankind as a dualistic bargain with men who professed to be Christian. According to this belief, before the fall, God related to his creatures through the covenant of works, which saw man's obedience and attention to devotional activity as the prerequisite for an eternal life with God in paradise. But after Adam and Eve's sin, the time span before Christ's coming described in the Old Testament, and His subsequent crucifixion, death, resurrection, and redemption of humankind, God reverted to a covenant of grace, a bargain with man that stipulated that He would choose some men to be saved solely because of Christ's sacrifice and through the grace that was generated by it. The corollary was that any individual man could do nothing to effect his own salvation, but all men had to trust totally in God so that some of them would be saved. Thus, the covenant of works was abolished and no longer were the faithful urged to use prayer, meditation, and doing good to others to convince God of their worth, practices that had continued to be essential aspects of Roman Catholicism and could even, in some cases, be purchased by donations to the Church. Instead, searching for evidence of one's own salvation became a chief, if not the only, reason for being of the Puritan Christian.

The movement of Puritanism to the New World added to this traditional interpretation of biblical directives about man's salvation with the vision that John Winthrop gave the first generation of New England Puritans of a "city on a hill" that was meant by God to be an example to the rest of the world of what a perfectly covenanted Christian community could be like. This communal vision sustained the original Puritans and allowed that first generation to conquer, or at least endure, the wilderness; this vision also emerges from much of Taylor's poetry. This dream, actually dating from the days of British Puritan exile in Germany and the Netherlands but not fully pursued until the establishment of the American colonies, is the need to knit the community together and ensure its legitimate sacredness by insisting that each potential church member—and consequently member of the theocratic community—deliver a public profession of faith that would ensure the others, as much as possible on earth, that every member of the church was operating under the terms of the covenant of grace. An additional corollary was that no other churches were allowed to operate within the community, so that the government and the church could have complete control over the social and spiritual life of people in the colony (Morgan 121). Thus, until the public relation of the conversion experience was made, an early Puritan person in the American colonies was a virtual outcast from all activities in the community. From 1646 on in the Massachusetts colonies and a few years later in the Connecticut and New Haven colonies, however, all residents were required to attend church services, although they had no actual standing in the community until their public relation was accepted. The theory behind this change was that sermons were one means of channeling saving grace to those whom God had elected (Morgan 123) and thus more people would ascertain their conversion, and the number of church members would be more likely to increase.

At first, this required profession of faith served the same purpose as an oath, pledging the individual Puritan's allegiance to the doctrines of the fledgling denomination (Morgan 40–41). This eventually evolved into a public account of one's actual conversion experience, the public relation peculiar to the congregations of New England. The necessity to account verbally for one's worthiness to be a church member was first suggested in the writings of the British Puritan Henry Ainsworth as a way to counter the excessive traditional dependence on the covenant of works, what Taylor himself is referring to in *Gods Determinations* when he pictures certain men's pride in their own endeavors (Morgan 56). By the time this religious practice of the confession of faith got to American shores, to sustain the original vision of the perfect Christian community, the necessity of recounting one's conversion experience in front of a panel of church elders and having it and one's resulting church membership accepted publicly became a major part of the New England Puritan experience, most likely beginning in non-Separating Puritan colonies like that at Massachusetts Bay. Colonial Puritan life had a secure focus on this dual project: ascertaining the moment of assurance in one's own conscience and then creating a public narrative of that assurance so that others in the community could not only share in your joy, but judge its legitimacy as well and then admit you to church membership or, in later days, allow you finally to participate in the Lord's Supper. Taylor's own "Foundation Day Sermon" illustrates that the Puritans found biblical precedent in the Old Testament accounts of ceremonial worship as well as the actions of Old Testament personages, including David and Solomon, for the public nature of this relation. In the sermon, Taylor also cites John the Baptist and several of the New Testament epistles to show that the practice was also sanctioned in Jesus's days on earth, and then refers to the early Christians and church fathers who continued the practice. As with many other ordinances and religious practices in Puritan worship, the public relation was thus thought to be sanctioned by God due to its presence in the scriptures.

Many, if not most, of the conversion accounts that led to full church membership were recorded in the church records of respective congregations, and themselves make up a body of early American literature. As time went on, the text of these narratives became formalized, revealing exactly how Puritan doctrine characterized the progress of the elect soul toward evidence of its salvation. A pattern can be seen in legions of conversion narratives that is similar to that of Taylor's own narrative recorded in the Westfield church records. Most narratives start with acknowledgment of the individual's good religious upbringing that was often ignored or taken for granted and subject to occasional backsliding, until a personal problem or even a catastrophe focused the attention of the

Christian on his or her need for God. Patricia Caldwell points out additionally that the voyage to the New World and the hardships the American Puritans encountered added a characteristic focus to this part of the narrative on the convert's sinfulness and the suffering undergone in the wilderness that was attributed not to the natural difficulty of settling in an undeveloped land, but to the grievousness of the individual's life of sin (136). Once the convert's attention was turned away from worldliness and toward prayer, meditation, and a surer seeking after Christ, however, the penitent would eventually come to a realization of his or her totally helpless state, the ineffectuality of those devotional acts to change God's mind, and the resultant dependence on Jesus alone. At this point, if the person was among the Elect, he or she would experience the infusion of irresistible grace. One of the highlights of the public relation was the account of how the person ascertained this infusion, which was often precisely felt, most often during a worship service or during private devotion, but sometimes while performing an activity as mundane as sweeping the floor. The final few words of the narrative expressed how the convinced Christian still had to struggle with doubt and was never absolutely certain that the experience had been real (Morgan 91). Additionally, as Caldwell observes, the language of the Bible was as much a part of the typical New England conversion narrative as it is of Taylor's poetry (168). Caldwell notes that this dependence on biblical imagery, structure, and patterns in a profession of faith is peculiarly American (171). If a person's narrative followed this pattern, moreover, it almost always was accepted by the church elders, and he or she became a full church member (Morgan 72). Taylor reflects this pattern not only in his own conversion narrative, but also in the experiences of his fictional Christians facing the Last Judgment in *Gods Determinations*, and his own spiritual experience described in the meditative poetry.

New Israelite Consciousness

Taylor's poetry also shares what Sacvan Bercovitch has called the New Israelite consciousness that emerges as another major facet of the American Puritan experience. This self-perception of the New England colonists is based on their familiarity with typology and their tendency to extend it out of the Bible and make it pertinent to their own situation. Recent research has suggested that this Puritan view of the self had roots in earlier British Protestantism and developed into the eighteenth century to shape the consciousness of the emerging United States of America

(Delbanco 87). Taylor himself believed in an extended use of strict typological theory that allowed him to see a historical and theological continuum (the same world view that was the impetus for the composition
of the "Metrical History of Christianity") that related not only Old Testament personae, events, and symbols to Christ but also connected biblical reality to himself and the entire Puritan colony (Rowe 1–2).

This way of thinking was productive of much of the language that
emerges from Puritan text that shows the writers identifying themselves
and their community with the Hebrews whose story dominates the Book
of Exodus in the Bible. References to themselves as Israelites, their communal experience of wandering in a wilderness to evade persecution for
their religious beliefs, and God's faithfulness toward them even in times
of backsliding appear in colonial histories, sermons, and poetry. For example, the Puritan preacher John Cotton cites the fate of the straying
Israelites as a warning to his New England congregation in one of his
sermons: "When the Israelites liked not the soil, grew weary of the Ordinances, and forsook the Worship of God, and said, *What part have we
in David?* After this . . . He waxed weary of them, and cast them out of
His sight" (Cotton, *Gods Promise* 16–17). Matching wilderness to wilderness, this analogy allowed the Puritans to see themselves—even in the
darkest times—in a God-sanctioned mode and gave them license to
model their society based on the bits and pieces of theocratic evidence
presented in the pages of the Bible, particularly the Old Testament. It
also allowed them, again through the process of typology, to Christologize
the Old Testament and more clearly see Old Testament figures such as
David as models for Christians.

This frame of mind is no doubt what allows Taylor to identify not only
some of the subjects of his elegies, but also himself, with certain biblical
personages. This sort of identification, a quasi-typological equation between significant figures of the Old Testament and important ministers
and magistrates of New England, was common, particularly in the structure of the New England elegy. Jeffrey Hammond notes the communal
solidification intended to result from this sort of identification ("Diffusing" 169). Although Barbara Lewalski's contention that Taylor identifies
himself with Christ in the typology poems seems beyond what a Puritan
would do, it is clear that Taylor's chief identification with these figures
that is revealed in his poetic canon is with the poets of the Bible, particularly David the psalmist and Solomon, as the author of the Canticles
(Lewalski 406–7, 413; Hammond, *Sinful Self* 223–24; Rowe 230). Because
biblical exegesis that Taylor would have been familiar with indicated that

Solomon himself was an elderly man when he penned the Song of Songs, Taylor's use of this biblical book for his later poems seems particularly apt (Davis, *Reading* 190).

Karen Rowe also sees as one of the central metaphors of the *Preparatory Meditations* the exodus journey made by the Hebrews in the Old Testament (230). Clearly, the typical Puritan preoccupation with self-examination of the state of one's soul and the journey through the stages of justification, sanctification, and glorification is an internal, spiritual parallel to the Israelites' wanderings in the wilderness and their eventual arrival in the Promised Land. Not only was the Book of Exodus a guide for their wilderness experience, but the Book of Psalms was often exegetically treated as a poetic rendering of the history of the Old Testament wilderness people, with several psalms focusing on wilderness wandering, either historically in relation to the exodus or personally concerning David's experiences of hardship. Through both these Old Testament books, the Puritans were made to see how God dealt with His people during a wilderness experience and thus these texts served to guide them spiritually. It was a natural outgrowth of this identification with both the Israelites in general and the Hebrew poet David in particular for Taylor to use the Book of Psalms—not only a devotional guide for wilderness people but also a poetic book—as his model for the *Preparatory Meditations*, and to view himself, if only privately, as the sweet singer of the New Israel.

The Communion Controversy

Another facet of the New England Puritan culture that had a major impact on the progress of Taylor's poetry was his involvement in the important controversy concerning the gradual liberalization of the Puritan sacraments, baptism and the Lord's Supper or communion. The manuscript of Taylor's eight sermons of 1694, edited by Norman S. Grabo as the *Treatise concerning the Lord's Supper*, is contained along with other documents relating to the controversy in the Boston Public Library Prince collection. Taylor wrote these sermons at the same time he was writing the beginning poems of the Second Series of his *Preparatory Meditations*, although it seems more likely that Taylor composed Meditations 2.102–11—all headed by biblical verses from Matthew 26 that relate to the Last Supper—in direct response to the Northampton minister Solomon Stoddard's relaxation of standards related to Puritan sacramental theology. Karen Rowe even believes these latter poems, written during 1711–12, are paralleled by other sermons that have been lost (Rowe 168). She finds evidence for this particularly in a shift of tone from earlier Meditations to what she describes as a more "preacherly" and even defensive tone (206–7), which is surely reflected in the highly doctrinal nature of these ten poems. Thomas Davis also attributes the shift in tone between the First and Second Series at least partially to Taylor's reaction to Stoddard's ideas (*Reading* 121). It was Stoddard's sermon on Galatians 3.1 in 1690, several years before Taylor concluded the First Series of the *Preparatory Meditations*, that made the first move toward the identification of the eucharist as a converting ordinance, that is, as effective as prayer, listening to sermons, and meditating privately in preparing the as yet unconverted Puritan for the infusion of grace into his or her soul (Davis and Davis, *Church Records* xxiii–xxiv).

In Meditations 2.102–11, only the headnote of Meditation 2.107 does not use verses from Matthew 26, using instead a verse from Luke: "Lu 22.19. This do in remembrance of Mee," which is nonetheless also related to Christ's words at the Last Supper. Donald Stanford published part of this sequence—specifically Meditations 2.104–9 and 2.111—in a 1956 issue of the *Yale University Library Gazette*, as a way of proving that Taylor espoused an orthodox view of the Supper as a seal of the Puritan covenant of grace, meant only for those who were already converted (Hammond, *Fifty* 19). The legalistic imagery in Meditation 2.102 sets the same tone of concern that Taylor voices in the *Treatise*. In fact, all but the last verse of the poem recounts orthodox Puritan doctrine about the purpose of the sacrament, the nature of the covenant of grace, and Christ's sacrificial role in its institution. The next Meditation, 2.103, gets even more legalistic as it attempts to recount the process of the two covenants, Jesus' sacrifice, and the resulting dispensation of grace in twelve tortuous verses that dwell on typology to justify the use of ceremonies in the New Testament and afterwards as "Signification" of the seal of grace. Finally, in Meditation 2.104, Taylor's poetry becomes more metaphorical about the Supper, as he applies the image of God as the baker of the saving bread that we first see in Meditation 1.8. Later in the poem, Taylor makes his point more clearly: "This Feast is no Regenerating fare. / But food for those Regenerate that are." By the time he gets to Meditation 2.106, however, Taylor has returned to the *Preparatory Meditations'* central concerns of his own desire to experience the assurance of saving grace, promises to praise if conversion is achieved, and frustration at the limits of human language to offer the devotion that God deserves. Thus, gradually, Taylor is able to integrate his constant, more personal themes with his interest in this major doctrinal issue. In Meditation 2.108, he depicts himself as actually invited to the banquet that he feared he could not participate in when he wrote "The Reflexion" nearly thirty years earlier. He even takes the opportunity to attack the Catholics and their false doctrine of transubstantiation as well as the heretical Puritans who would treat the sacrament as a converting ordinance, two groups whom he puts essentially in the same category. In Meditation 2.110, he further declares about the Lord's Supper banquet: "And with these Guests I am invited to't / And this rich banquet makes me thus a Poet." Subsequently, the latter six poems in this sequence end with his ubiquitous promise to sing and to write praises if he is numbered among the Elect who deserve to receive the Supper.

Taylor's view of sacramental theology carefully followed the development of New England Puritan belief in the place and purpose of baptism and communion. Both sacraments were initially looked upon as seals of the covenant of grace, available only to those who had ascertained their election, because they reinforced the moment of assurance of conversion and—as Taylor depicts in "The Experience" so vividly—were the only times when a Puritan could come close to a spiritual union with Christ. Taylor, in fact, saw the elect Christian's participation in the Lord's Supper experience to position him closer to the spirit of God and to give him a foretaste of heaven, which only the saved should be able to experience (Grabo, *Taylor* 17; Gatta 83–84). But even before Taylor had arrived in the Massachusetts Bay colony, the Puritans had been beset by the consequences of this belief. The custom in England before the migration was to baptize children of converted church members, and then nurture them in the paths that would lead to their conversion. On the shores of New England, the Puritan colonies continued this practice, assuming that the children of saved Christians would necessarily seek their own conversion experience when they came of age. Thus, baptism as a sacrament meant only for the converted quickly went by the wayside, which only seems logical if a denomination practices infant baptism. According to the Cambridge Platform of 1648, only the Lord's Supper was to be denied to the baptized children of current church members; they were to participate in all church activities and be subject to church discipline (Morgan 126). But the real problem with this system arose when the second generation of baptized church members who had not yet undergone their conversion experience nevertheless married and began to have children. Because no deadline had been placed on the age by which a baptized-only church member had to experience and relate his or her conversion, the birth of the third generation sent Puritan divines into a quandary, because they saw the ultimate outcome as a church in which no one was saved, but only a descendent of someone who had related his or her conversion experience and had it accepted. The Synod of 1662, forced to come to terms with the fact that the number of truly converted Puritans was dwindling and the theocracy was faced with an insurmountable problem caused by biology, adopted the rules that troubled Taylor from his arrival in the New World, informally referred to as the Halfway Covenant, which concluded that children of baptized church members could still be members of the same church as their parents and, like their parents, were subject to the watchfulness and discipline of the elders of the church and urged to seek their conversion, but neither they nor their parents could receive communion until they had conversion experiences that were judged acceptable by the elders (Morgan 130–31). This measure allowed church membership to swell, and it also focused increased attention on the eucharist as the only remaining ordinance meant solely for the converted.

By the time Taylor became an important theological presence in the Massachusetts Bay and Connecticut Valley, baptism was totally downplayed as a seal of the covenant. In his "Foundation Day Sermon," Taylor even identifies baptism as a sacrament of initiation that would begin the Christian's search for the conversion experience that would allow him or her to partake legitimately, according to the principles of church discipline, of the Lord's Supper (Davis and Davis, *Church Records* xxii; Taylor, "Foundation" 125). The experience of the eucharist was at the covenant's center, which itself was at the center of the entire theological structure of Puritanism. Thus, to conduct one's religious life in a traditional Puritan manner, it was necessary to attend to one's relationship to this seal of the covenant. Furthermore, as minister, Taylor also needed to tend to the needs of the covenanted congregation he led. With this viewpoint in mind, it is easy to see why Stoddard's attempts to liberalize the sacrament of the eucharist and allow it to become a converting ordinance was such a shock to those like Taylor who were interested in preserving the traditional structure of American Puritanism.

In his introduction to Taylor's sermons, Norman Grabo outlines the five main reasons Taylor offers in the *Treatise concerning the Lord's Supper* in defense of his orthodox position on the sacrament (xiv–xviii). He states in no uncertain terms that the gift of the eucharist is a seal of the covenant of grace, the second covenant or "New Covenant" between God and man. Taylor also depicts this gift as a result of God's gracious will and intentions for man's life, and a sign of man's importance to his Creator, but made possible only through Christ's redemptive sacrifice. Taylor also points out that the sacrament is the last one that Christ establishes in the New Testament before His death and one that all faithful Christians have revered since the early Christian era, and consequently the best and most mature mark of a converted soul. He even uses the fact that Catholics, or the Papists as he calls them, view the eucharist as one of their seven sacraments as part of the proof of its high estimation throughout the whole history of the Christian religion, a departure from his usually scornful view of this denomination. Additionally, as he also evidences through the plot of *Gods Determinations*, Taylor views the eucharist as a chief frustration to Satan because it has paved a new path to heaven just when Satan was sure that sinful man was his. Finally, Taylor observes that, as God's tribute to man, the eucharist is meant only for visible saints, although its presence in church services does function as an inducement of desire for the unconverted to seek out evidence of their possible conversion in order to be accepted at the Supper with the rest of the visible saints. Taylor indeed states his belief in a sense of envy they would experience upon seeing the converted receive the sacrament that might motivate the unregenerate to more avidly seek their own conversion experiences (Gatta 87, 92).

As he clung to the orthodox position that to Taylor was the direct reason why the New England Puritans had consented to undergo the rigorous wilderness experience in the New World, and as he wrote long, mostly doctrinal defenses of this chief tenet of Puritanism, Taylor found himself increasingly in the minority, not only in his own congregation but throughout the Puritan settlements in New England. Taylor's meditative poetry conveys his belief that assurance of conversion could never be absolutely certain while the seeker was on earth, and this uncertainty gives power and impetus to his poetry. But congregations such as Stoddard's in the Connecticut Valley were quickly concluding from the same belief that it was impossible for anyone to discover saving faith, and thus it made no sense to withhold anything that might enhance spiritual life from dedicated believers. Thomas and Virginia Davis conclude that Stoddard's motivation for this departure from traditional theology was ironically the same as Taylor's to preserve it—the need to strengthen church discipline and assure the continuance of strong church membership (*Church Records* xxix–xxx). Edmund Morgan surmises that this intention to make people realize that they had to be vigilant always because they could never be totally assured of their own salvation also gave birth to the kind of "hellfire sermons" and revivalist mentality that Stoddard began and later Puritans like his grandson Jonathan Edwards continued,

ushering in the second wave of New England Puritanism that we call the
Great Awakening (147). Nevertheless, Taylor continued to deliver less
emotional and more Scripture-bound logical sermons to convince his
congregation of the importance of continuing to view the sacrament as
meant only for regenerate church members. At the same time, however,
his poetry may have become for Taylor a kind of retreat, a private way to
play with his particular gift of facility with language in the expression of
his orthodox concerns and his heartfelt beliefs as he began to see their
potency erode in his own community (Gatta 87).

For several years, it appeared that Taylor had remained silent except
for his private poetry, stewing about this matter within the confines of
Westfield, but Donald Stanford's discovery of the Thomas Prince collection of manuscripts in the Boston Public Library revealed more prose
documents written by Taylor in response to Stoddard that evidence indicates were distributed and read at the time they were written. Prince,
a New England Puritan minister who had received his B.A. from Harvard
in 1709, intended to write a book protesting the liberalization of the
sacraments, and collected all of Taylor's manuscripts that had been cir-
culating in response to Stoddard's writing and that of the Boston Mathers.
The book never materialized, and the manuscripts were eventually given
to the Boston Public Library by the deacons of Boston's Old South
Church, with the rest of Prince's papers. One notable inclusion in the
Prince collection was the manuscript of the sermon that Taylor had revised extensively since its original delivery on the Westfield church's
foundation day, newly entitled "A Particular Church Is Gods House."
Thomas and Virginia Davis surmise the revision is in the handwriting of
the early 1690s, placing it at the time when Stoddard began his overt
campaign to have the Lord's Supper named a converting ordinance
(*Church Records* 477). A survey of both sermons indicates the particular
direction that Taylor took in relation to the writing and preaching of
Stoddard.

Taylor retains much of the original sermon, including the statement of
the necessity of a public relation of one's conversion experience (although
he strengthens the message in the revision by referring to the scandal
that would be caused if the Puritan churches abandoned the public relation, as Stoddard wanted to do). Unlike in the original sermon, however, in the revised sermon Taylor also attacks the idea that the eucharist
could ever work for a person's conversion. He strengthens the jeremiad
quality of the sermon by reminding the reader of how far changes like

those that Stoddard wished to make departed from the original intentions of the earliest settlers (Davis and Davis, *Church Records* xxvii). In the first part of the sermon, Taylor adds passages that emphasize that every member of a Puritan congregation must be holy. He says: "For such as are not really Holy have no right to it, nor appetite after it, nor Power to eate thereof, nor Concoctive faculty to digest the same into nutriment" ("Revised" 295). This sentence enters the sermon without introduction that would connect it explicitly to the Lord's Supper, and Taylor next explores metaphors of food and drink as analogies for the necessities of the spirit. He continues to insist that nobody will get nourishment from the eucharist unless they are previously saved. Several times he tackles more extensively the Halfway Covenant, stating that halfway members may attend church but "they are not to be laid in as Matter fit for the Essentiall form of the Building" (297), a metaphor he uses for full church membership. He clearly states that there really is no difference between them and those who are totally outside the church when it comes to the necessity of delivering a public relation of the conversion experience before participating in the eucharist. He proceeds by citing many historical precedents for the confession of faith as a prerequisite for, in many cases, baptism and the Lord's Supper, adding many more instances as proof beyond those he recorded in the original sermon. Finally, about halfway through the sermon, he states outright: "That the Lords Supper is no Converting Ordinance" (319), and then proceeds to offer defenses for this position, stating that according to scriptural precedent, baptism, full church participation and visible holiness, and careful self-examination of the mental faculties leading to a discernment of the presence of saving faith are necessary before anyone should be able to receive communion. He also argues that the Lord's Supper is part of formal worship that relates to the covenant of grace, as opposed to other converting ordinances, such as prayer and meditation, that spring out of one's human nature, and that the sacrament is so intimate that no unsaved Christian should be permitted to partake of it. He then cites several church fathers who also declare that participation in the Supper is not meant to convert the unregenerate, and then confirms the point by noting that the Roman Catholics do allow anyone to partake of the sacrament, a point disputed by such early Reformation leaders as Martin Luther. Although this sermon was never published or, as far as we can tell, delivered—it comprises ninety pages in the Davis text—it clearly illustrates, as do many of the Second Series meditative poems, Taylor's position on this last vestige of the old New England way.

LITERARY INFLUENCES

The Puritan View of Original Literature

Although no one text composed in Taylor's time delineates the Puritan attitude toward literary composition, the deprecation with which Taylor often writes about his own poetry and his ability to compose arises from an elemental distrust of human language that is part of the general Puritan reaction to writing, a definite irony in the lives of people so tied to the text of the Bible and the narratives of their own conversions. But the Puritans' tendency to put faith in the Word of God had the confusing effect of causing them to at once deify the verbal and distrust any language that was outside the realm of biblical relationship (Hammond, *Sinful Self* 9). This confusion often resulted in paralysis for the Puritan poet. The almost manic need for order that Thomas Davis posits leads Taylor to sequence almost all of his work may relate to this paralysis (*Reading* 140). Taylor's often studied stylistic roughness, his unconventional metaphors, his mixture of levels of diction, and his often inverted sentence structures and other syntactical abnormalities may also relate to the need to show he is a fallen man using a fallen language. As Michael Clark suggests, Taylor's enchantment with the Incarnation may stem from a belief that the Word made flesh also might somehow elevate the status of human language (74). Taylor's own writing about writing, woven especially throughout the meditative poetry, indicates that he does not always trust the way his own human talent processes language, but he does trust the Bible and so deliberately borrows his diction, form, imagery, and prosody from what he observes in his own reading of the holy book. In fact, Jeffrey Hammond refers to each poem in the *Preparatory Meditations* as "an internalized Bible in miniature" and Taylor's view of the Bible itself as "the great Poem" (*Sinful Self* 213–15), while Thomas Davis calls Taylor "one of the people of the Book" (*Reading* 202). Some critics view Taylor's dependence on the Bible as sapping any creativity that might have been possible. A clearer look at what Puritan literature does, however, reveals the rich legacy of the Word—its often sensuous imagery, the prosody of its poetic volumes, and the differences in style of its various books—as a positive influence not only on Taylor, but on the entire Puritan ability to create. Certainly in the Puritan mind, a dependence on and knowledge of the intricacies of biblical language would work to ensure that creative writing was not an activity that would damn the writer through an excess of pride in his own accomplishments. Biblically modeled language could anticipate what Taylor expresses in the later Meditations and the vale-

dictory poems, that only death and subsequent glorification would sanc-
tify human language and make it at last totally acceptable to the God
that the Puritan poet sought constantly to praise.

Both this last principle and the struggle Taylor went through to reach
it reflect the theory of the American Puritan mind toward human language. As evidenced, for example, by the set forms of prayer controversy
that inspired John Cotton to write the only aesthetic treatise in the New
England colonies, *Singing of Psalmes a Gospel Ordinance* (London 1647),
the Puritans' distrust of human language was offset by the belief that God
had sanctioned the words, figures, and poetic forms that were in the Bible.
And it wasn't only Puritans who believed this way. Many seventeenth-
century British devotional poets also modeled their work with a strict eye
on Protestant exegesis of the Bible and a careful use of the biblical techniques that Taylor also knew and used, including typology, emblem book
imagery, and Protestant meditative and sermon techniques (Lewalski
425).

Perhaps the strongest factor in the development of the informal aesthetic that guided Puritan composition was the theory and exegesis that
surrounded Puritan use of the Book of Psalms. As much as they distrusted
language, the Puritans did embrace music and it provided a bridge into
proper aesthetics. Although their interpretation of biblical worship practices required that they keep instrumental music separate from worship
in the meetinghouse, they still used instruments and song in private
home-based devotion and secular activities. The a cappella singing of
psalms also characterized all their worship services, as its use accompanied
by such instruments as violin and harpsichord enhanced their entertain-
ment at home. Puritan focus on the Book of Psalms as the source for all
church music gradually made it the center of not only their devotional
life, but of their informal prosodic theory, helpful because the psalms
existed both as hymns and poems, using both music and language.

As it had been in England, the Book of Psalms was used as a meditative
handbook in the Puritan American colonies that allowed the faithful to
structure their private devotion. The New Englanders' emphasis on the
practice of self-examination in meditation as a way to assess one's pattern
of progress toward discernment of individual spiritual fate was a major
impetus for their meditative writing, and David's penitence and faith as
expressed in his psalms gave them a viable, sanctioned pattern. In *Singing
of Psalmes a Gospel Ordinance*, John Cotton urges Puritans who would
write private meditations and poetry to compile these out of the words
of the psalter (15, 28–29). Later, in his *Psalterium Americanum* (Boston,

1718), the Puritan minister Cotton Mather also advises that the Psalms provide "the best Forms in the World for our Prayers" (iv–v). The relatively small amount of devotional poetry written in the Puritan colonies, including Taylor's work, also clearly uses psalmic imagery and form. Thus, the Puritans' love for and relative trust of music as an expression of devotion, as well as the presence of musical poems in the Old Testament, tempered somewhat their distrust of language.

Part of this use of the Psalms was deliberate modeling, but another part was a natural reaction to the internalizing of the Psalms and other parts of the Bible by members of the Puritan community. In all their daily activities, particularly in their constant hearing, speaking, and singing of the words of the Bible in meeting and prayer sessions, the Puritans built their vocabulary, their idioms, their maxims, and their everyday discourse on the words they heard and consumed. As Hammond notes, this caused them to experience "an inner expression of biblical pattern" (*Sinful Self* 17), feeding into the perception of themselves as New Israelites. The centrality of the singing of Psalms in church services and in private homes further imprinted the words on people's memories.

Based on their assumption that David is the speaking subject of the poems in the Book of Psalms, he also became for many Christians from early modern times on forward the voice of the Christian everyman caught in the familiar continuum between doubt and assurance of his own salvation. The literalism with which Protestants interpreted the Bible caused them to focus on David's humanity and regard him without question as the author of all the psalms. Thus, he could become a ready example to be used in sermons and treatises of an earthbound, even sinful believer who eventually becomes a praising saint. That David was in the Old Testament appears not to bother those commentators and exegetes, who use the process of Christology to allow them to see him as a model for Christians. The God he petitions and praises in the Old Testament is, for them, as much Christ as God the Father. David is consequently viewed throughout sixteenth- and seventeenth-century devotional literature as the foremost model for all meditative and pious exercises, from repentance to joyful praise, and by default becomes the model contemporary Protestant Christian used as a figure in much of this literature. As John Donne says in his sermon on Psalm 63.7: "David was not onely a cleare Prophet of Christ himselfe, but a Prophet of every particular Christian; he foretells what I, what any shall doe, and suffer, and say" (Simpson 94).

It is only one step further for David to become the model of the pious author. He is described most often in commentaries as a conscious artist who models songs for the glory of God. The psalter was thus looked upon as an aesthetic feat in both its form and meaning, and Christian poets were expected to depend on the psalter as their aesthetic guide. Additionally, David was viewed as both a struggling human being like any devotional poet who was attempting to reach God through his gift of poetry and an inspired prophet whose words became sanctioned as he uttered them. Because of this, other devotional artists could find sanction for their work and for their own identity as poets by imitating what David had created.

For the New England Puritan, David assumes the additional identity of the regenerate soul, a role that acquires a specificity in colonial writings that it does not have in earlier British exegesis and meditative literature. Any language in the psalter that hints at a conversion, such as the purification ritual David undergoes in Psalm 51, becomes centralized in New England colonial writing, and the very existence of the Book of Psalms as part of the Bible indicates that David's salvation was assured. That he also was a type of Christ reinforced his model role as the prototypical regenerate soul that other Christians should imitate.

As the Puritan experiment began to deteriorate throughout the 1680s and 1690s, the more orthodox writers also began to view David as a model for the few saints who had related their conversion experiences and thus were privileged to participate in the Lord's Supper. As admission to communion became the center of controversy in the colonies, David became a model of suitability to receive the Supper because his conversion is first assured. Cotton Mather in his 1690 treatise *A Companion for Communicants,* for example, cites David as an indication that church membership and the ordinance of the Supper are solely for those who have been certified as members of the Elect, noting that David in Psalm 101 says that liars and deceivers are not permitted entrance to his house (41–42). Mather then attributes this kind of falsehood to those who would receive the Supper when they were not yet assured of their own spiritual fate. Edward Taylor himself, in his "Foundation Day Sermon" and more emphatically in the revised version of this sermon, uses Psalm 66, in which David speaks of God's revelation to him, as an example of the public relation of a conversion experience.

These identities for David that were so particular to the New England Puritan colony and the theological issues that it faced may have reinforced for Taylor the appropriateness of David and the verses that he wrote as a model for his own poetic work. We know that he actually paraphrased some of the Psalms in 1674–75 and again in the 1680s, and

Thomas Davis surmises that this work may have profoundly influenced his decision to begin the *Preparatory Meditations* (*Reading* 23; Rowe 271). Davis, in fact, posits that Meditation 7 of the First Series, which has as its headnote "Ps. 45.2. Grace in thy lips is poured out"—the first of only three headnotes from the Book of Psalms—is the actual beginning of the *Preparatory Meditations* in Taylor's mind, modeled very specifically after that biblical book (*Reading* 72). Taylor readily admits in Meditation 2.2 that his *Preparatory Meditations* is his attempt to follow in David's biblical footsteps: "I'le hang my love then on his [Christ's] heart, and sing / New Psalms on Davids Harpe to thee and him." Thus the Book of Psalms is the central part of the Bible's words and structures that influences Taylor, provides him with informal aesthetic principles, and allows him to continue composing original poems through all the decades of his adult life.

Typology

Another biblical source that becomes a literary influence for Taylor, particularly in Meditations 2.1–30, is biblical typology. This exegetical technique originates in attempts to harmonize the events of the Old Testament with those of the New Testament, to see a sense of conscious Christian purpose in the entire Bible from beginning to end. In the discourse of this religious linguistic practice, people, events, and objects in the Old Testament serve as foreshadowing for events in the life of Jesus (the antitype), or attributes of His person. Books about typology, most notably *The Figures or Types of the Old Testament* by Samuel Mather and *Christ Revealed; or the Old Testament Explained* by Thomas Taylor, were being published or reissued during the seventeenth century and typological exegesis was very much in vogue among Christians at the time that Taylor began to compose his book of meditative poetry (Rowe 74, Lowance 90). Jeffrey Hammond suggests that Taylor uses the typology sequence in the *Preparatory Meditations* to show off his ability to deal successfully with not only the words, but also the mysteries and techniques of the Bible, and his grasp of its overall unity (*Sinful Self* 219–20).

As Rowe describes Taylor's use of the structure, he generally begins a poem by making a statement about the typal relationship followed by an explanation of the type; he then parallels the type with Christ, and ends the poem with an application to his own spiritual situation (Rowe 140). Meditation 2.7 is a good example of this technique. The poem focuses on the biblical Joseph as a type of Christ. Taylor actually begins this poem

by expressing his need to concentrate on a type in order to shore up his
spirit and make his writing better. He then begins to unfold poetically
the typal relationship:

> Is Josephs glorious shine a Type of thee?
>   How bright art thou? He Envi'de was as well.
> And so was thou. He's stript, and pick't, poore hee,
>   Into the pit. And so was thou.

This paralleling of Joseph with Christ continues through five verses, and
in the last verse, Taylor compares his own "dull . . . Skin" with the brightly
colored coat Joseph wore, which itself is a type of Christ's brightness. He
then asks Christ to give him such a coat, as well as to "Scoure thou my
pipes" so that Taylor can continue to sing praises that are suitable.

We do not know why Taylor, in 1693, ended the First Series of Meditations with his forty-ninth poem, based on a verse from Matthew: "Matt.
25.21: The joy of thy Lord," and began the first poem of the Second
Series with a meditation based on the typologically charged passage from
Collossians: "Col. 2.17. Which are Shaddows of things to come and the
body is Christs." The themes of the poems are nearly identical, and typically Taylor: an admission of his own sinfulness and unworthiness coupled with a plea to Christ to ignore his bad traits and lead him more
solidly in righteous ways, ending with a promise to praise if Christ grants
this request. The significant difference is that in the third stanza of Meditation 2.1, he turns from this personal theme to a discussion of the use
of typology. The next twenty-nine poems of the Second Series then proceed to explore this exegetical practice. Once in awhile, a poem in the
Second Series goes back to the more central theme of Taylor's unworthiness and doubt about his own salvation, but for the most part the poems
explore and expand metaphors connected to standard type–antitype connections. This makes the poems, even within the ubiquitous stanzaic
structure, even more rigid, because the pattern of typological connection
is highly structured and monolithic, as opposed to the variety of prosodic
and linguistic elements Taylor could find in the Psalms and other biblical
books by which to enhance previous Meditations.

Several critics theorize that Taylor felt the need to turn to established
religious doctrine in order to regain the equilibrium necessary to begin
again to write successful poetry after the encounter with his own sin that
preoccupies the poems at the end of the First Series. Thomas Davis points

out that, in addition, Taylor's first wife, Elizabeth, died in 1689 while he was writing the final few poems of the First Series, and this death focused his attention on the significant differences between spiritual and carnal approaches to life. Davis theorizes that because Taylor realized that his own poetry and poetic talent were part of his earthly existence, he perhaps felt it necessary to decrease his originality and lyricism and model his verses more deliberately after acceptable biblical precedent in order to make them more spiritual and thus more conducive to his own search for salvation (*Reading* 116–18). Rowe goes further to suggest that Taylor sees a connection between the process of typology and the dualistic state of his own spiritual reality, which has been his central theme all along (22; Hammond, *Sinful Self* 203–4). This connection is borne out even earlier by Meditations 1.14–18, which deal with Christ's typal relationship to the Old Testament figures of prophet, priest, and king. The Meditation on "Heb. 4:14. A Great High Priest" is numbered 14.15 and uses the imagery of the Old Testament sacrificial altar to figure typologically Christ's death and ascension. Also, in the same Meditation, Taylor pictures his own "Lumpish Heart" and "Chilly Numbd Affections," but also expresses hope that he will eventually fly to Christ "When thy Warm Sun my frozen Lake unlocks." The juxtaposition of these features of the poem indicates that Taylor not only sees typology as a more sanctioned model for poetry than his own religious affections, but also that he connects the two.

Secular Influences

But the Bible with the various literary patterns that it offers, while constituting the major influence on Taylor's poetry, was not the only one. His training in the classics at Harvard—a staple of the seventeenth-century college curriculum—is also evident in the structuring of his verses, although in a relatively minor way. Perhaps this classicism is more apparent in Taylor's elegies, themselves a classical form. Jeffrey Hammond—who has written at length on the Puritan elegy—believes that Taylor uses classical structuring as a consolation device ("Diffusing" 172). Jane Eberwein also notes that many of the techniques he uses in the meditative poetry are classical. The biblical technique of antithesis that is ubiquitous in Taylor's poetry is also a classical figure, for which Eberwein uses the term hyperbole (69). Additionally, several other prosodic features of Taylor's poetry that appear to be modeled on the prosody of the Bible also have cognates in classical rhetorical techniques.

Several critics have also seen similarities between Taylor's poetry and that of the British metaphysicals, such as John Donne and George Herbert, using the seminal 1947 work by Rosemund Tuve, *Elizabethan and Metaphysical Imagery: Renaissance Poetics and Twentieth-Century Critics*, as their basis.[1] One of the first biographical descriptions of Taylor as a poet in James D. Hart's 1941 edition of the *Oxford Companion to American Literature* defines him as a metaphysical, an identification maintained in the 1983 fifth edition of the *Companion* and as recently as the 1995 sixth edition, which was revised and expanded by Phillip W. Leininger. Despite the numerous biblical source studies that seemed to indicate otherwise, Hart and Leininger still put Taylor in "the direct line" of such English metaphysicals as Herbert and Richard Crashaw (654). Taylor's obvious and ubiquitous use of the conceit and what Karl Keller terms Taylor's habit of "catechresis," or the far-fetched analogies that characterize the conceit, are clear features of British metaphysical poetry (Keller, *Example* 184). These, his use of erotic imagery to depict the union of the soul with Christ (Delbanco 140–42), and his obeisance to poetic "decorum" (Scheick 147–48) are all aspects of the poetry of the British metaphysicals. Early Taylor critics such as Kenneth Murdock even express belief that Taylor kept his poetry unpublished just because he was too emotionally and artistically attached to metaphysical technique and imagery, seeing this attachment as an embarrassment to his espousals of orthodox Puritanism.

The absence of any books of poetry by contemporary British devotional poets in Taylor's library, however, poses a dilemma for twentieth-century critics. In his introduction to Taylor's diary, Francis Murphy indicates that the Puritans in the New England colonies preferred the more baroque and devotional poetry of writers like Francis Quarles and Guilliaume du Bartas to that of such writers as John Donne and Andrew Marvell (12). Additionally, all the features of Taylor's poetry that are regularly used as reasons to brand him uniquely American are also, as Albert Gelpi has established, counter to the tendencies of metaphysical poetry (23). Although the same provocativeness of imagery is certainly present in John Donne's poetry, for example, the roughness of Taylor's rhythm and the homeliness of some of his metaphors make him different from the court-affiliated poets who are considered the British metaphysicals. The similarities that label Taylor "metaphysical" may reach beyond this identification to some of the larger habits of post-Renaissance discourse.

NOTE

1. Hammond traces the history of criticism that identifies Taylor as metaphysical or baroque beginning with the work of William B. Goodman and Harold S. Jantz (*Fifty* 12–15). See also Lewalski 388; Keller, *Example* 172; Gatta 12; and Eberwein 68.

5   Ideas

THE MYSTERY OF THE INCARNATION

From the beginning of the lyrical First Series of the *Preparatory Meditations*, Taylor articulates his central theme, a commonplace of Christianity, and an idea that allows him to be hopeful throughout his poetry and much of his prose—his absolute amazement at Christ's gift of the Incarnation, or what some critics refer to as the hypostatic union. This central manifestation of the being of the Divine in the human world, which Taylor often refers to as "Theanthropy," in Taylor's view permits man to undertake the *imitatio Christi*, that is, to model his own existence on Christ's life and the virtues that He showed while on earth. Even more significantly, this gift of God to man exists as a promise that the body and the soul may be antithetical, but they are not in a state of total disconnection. From the first verse of Meditation 1.1, Taylor's emotional reaction to this central mystery of the Christian experience is clear:

> What Love is this of thine, that Cannot bee
>   In thine Infinity, O Lord, Confinde,
> Unless it in thy very Person see,
>   Infinity, and Finity Conjoyn'd?
>   What hath thy Godhead, as not satisfide
>   Marri'de our Manhood, making it its Bride?

Taylor's absolute amazement that God would condescend to assume a human form that Taylor's Calvinist theology told him was marred, sinful, and lowly adds much emotional power, especially to the early Meditations.[1] In the fourth poem of the First Series of Meditations, "The Experience," Taylor appears to reveal that a vision of the Incarnation was actually the substance of the conversion experience that is described in the poem:

> Most strange it was! But yet more strange that shine
>   Which filld my Soul then to the brim to spy
> My Nature with thy Nature all Divine
>   Together joyn'd in Him thats Thou, and I.
>   Flesh of my Flesh, Bone of my Bone. There's run
>   Thy Godhead, and my Manhood in thy Son.

This concentration on the theme of the Incarnation is what gives the first half of the First Series of Meditations its sense of joy. In Taylor's mind, furthermore, the mystery of the Incarnation is intricately related to another of his central concerns, the institution of the Lord's Supper, where God also has condescended to give man a taste of the living bread that is His son and where the human and divine natures connect in a similar sense to the consubstantiation present at the offering of the bread and wine (Davis, *Reading* 78; Schweitzer 86). This, of course, gives him even more reason to continue to insist later in his life that the Supper can only be given to the regenerate.

Ivy Schweitzer offers an interesting surmise that Meditation 2.96 answers Meditation 1.1 (107). This latter poem, one of the most provocative in the Canticles sequence, does return to the theme of ardent love and the imagery of light and flame that characterize the first Meditation. It also uses the technique of interrogation that Taylor uses in Meditation 1.1. Using as its headnote "Cant. 1.2. Let him kiss me with the Kisse of his mouth," Meditation 2.96 furthermore uses the erotic imagery that Taylor often employs when expressing his hopes for salvation or, more importantly, his ecstasy at the thought that the Incarnation has made heaven possible for him.

Although he incorrectly attempts to tie Taylor's delight in the Incarnation to a sense of true medieval mysticism, Norman S. Grabo establishes that a discourse about the transformative power of the Incarnation for sinful man was extant in Puritan New England during Taylor's lifetime, with one important representative text being Increase Mather's *The Mystery of Christ*, which establishes the hierarchical anomaly in the Great Chain of Being that so amazes Taylor, as in Meditation 2.44: "Oh! Dignifide Humanity indeed: / Divinely person'd: almost Deifide." Grabo makes a point to underscore the word "almost," however, to reestablish that Taylor, even in his estimation, is not as thorough-going a mystic as St. John of the Cross (*Taylor* 44–45).

Parts of the Bible that Taylor particularly prized because they spoke about the Incarnation included the Song of Songs, the New Testament verses that focus on Christ as mediator and advocate, and any Old Testament typology (Hambrick-Stowe 57). All of these become major models for parts of Taylor's own poetry. William J. Scheick also observes that Taylor's delight in the earlier poems is tied to the Augustinian belief that the Incarnation is the rejuvenation of the prelapsarian union between two other entities often in a state of antithesis—nature and grace (21). So the mystery takes on universal importance, not just for Taylor personally, but for every Puritan who realized that his own degraded carnal body could become glorified due to Christ's change of that sinful body into one that is redeemed (Gelpi 35–37).

The connection of the Incarnation—the Word made Flesh—to language is also made explicit in Taylor's poetry. Scheick has suggested an enrichment of this theme in Taylor's mind, facilitated by the possibility of a parallel between Jesus as God's attempt to communicate to man the essence of His creative Self, and Taylor's own identity as an artist (38, 97). In Meditation 1.7, for example, the first language mentioned is that of Christ, "That Golden Mint of Words," which is used metaphorically to describe His saving act, thus equating communication with redemption. The last line of the poem, however, clearly asks for the grace-tinctured language to be translated into Taylor's soul: "Thy Bottle make my Soule, Lord, it [the Liquid Gold of Christ's words] to hold." This consequently becomes the spirit in which Taylor continues to write, often expressing hope that his words will be made acceptable by the Word and at other times promising Christ innumerable praises once Taylor gets to heaven.

The Incarnation is a favorite Taylor idea throughout his body of work, not just in the early Mediations. As late as Meditation 2.158, he is still marveling at the hypostatic union:

> Thy Glory Lord all other glory blinds.
>   The glory of thy Nature pure Divine.
> The glory that thy Human Nature joyns,
>   Out shines all mortall glory that doth shine.

Additionally, his focus in the incomplete "Harmony of the Gospels" is, according to Thomas and Virginia Davis, another attempt to show the conjunction of the human and divine natures of Christ (*Harmony* 1: xxxiv–xxxv). The *Christographia* sermons also concentrate on the attributes of Christ, which Taylor sees as centered in the hypostatic union. Grabo observes in his introduction to Taylor's sermons that, as a whole, they attempt to depict Christ in detail so Puritans may correctly undertake the *imitatio Christi* (xix).

Taylor also focuses in the *Christographia* sermons, on how the combination of Christ's two natures makes Him the perfect advocate for man (xxii). This becomes the theme of the Meditations in the Second Series that are referred to as the "Christographia" poems. After the first Canticles Meditation but before the sequence becomes full-blown, Taylor includes a number of poems that relate to the sermons in his *Christographia*. There is some disagreement about which of the poems actually parallel the sermon collection, as Christ is such a constant theme throughout the *Preparatory Meditations*. Norman S. Grabo and Karen Rowe identify Meditations 2.42–56, whose headnotes actually correspond to the scriptural topics of the sermons, as those that belong to this sequence. But Thomas Davis mentions the dates of the "Christographia" poems as 1699–1704, which means the poems called "Christographia" could begin as early as 2.31 and as late as 2.61. Of those that Grabo identifies, the biblical headnotes that give the theme to sermon and poem match exactly in twelve of the fourteen cases. Most of the poems from these years explore aspects of Christ's being, as do the prose sermons. Barbara Lewalski has observed that they render metaphorically what the sermons argue logically (414), a connection that other critics have posited about the relationship between Taylor's prose and poems in general.

Within the "Christographia" sequence, a number of poems also deal with headnotes and imagery from the Gospel of John and other New Testament books that are based on the love of Christ and its power to redeem man. This gospel had been singled out by John Calvin as different from the other gospels because it concentrates more abstractly and almost exclusively on Christ's attributes and his dual nature, rather than on the historical life of Jesus (Davis and Davis, *Harmony* 1: xv). Although this attitude was what caused Calvin to leave John's Gospel out of his harmony (the first major Protestant example of a harmony of the gospels), it was what gave Taylor the impetus to use the biblical book in his meditative poetry. These "Christographia" poems, while focusing on the same theme as his earliest meditative poetry in the First Series, take a more staid and doctrinal position on the mystery of the Incarnation. His perception of the great sacrifice of Christ taking on a human body that will subsequently be tortured and killed produces this verse:

Thy Body is a Building all like mine,
   In Matter, Form, in Essence, Properties.
Yet Sin ne'er toucht it, Grace ne'er ceast in't'shine.
   It, though not Godded, next to th'Godhead lies.
   This honour have I, more than th'Angells bright.
   Thy Person, and my Nature do Unite. (Med. 2.42)

Compared to the ecstatic verses in Meditation 1.1, these lines betray the more cautious and less lyrical Taylor of the Second Series, even when he takes the doctrinal issues and applies them personally.

Taylor also expresses his characteristic theme of the insufficiency of language in the "Christographia" poems (Davis, *Reading* 163). Meditation 2.42 promises Christ that He would be given better words if Taylor was able to muster them, and then ends with a typical bargain request: "My Soule shall sing Thanksgiving unto thee, / If thou wilt tune it to thy praise in mee." The next Meditation tackles the same subject from the beginning, returning to the self-deprecation that has not appeared this vehemently since the end of the First Series. In the first verse, Taylor images himself as tongue-tied and in a trance, unable to proceed with his poetic gift. But in the second verse, we see Taylor begin to move toward blaming language itself, rather than his own lack of ability: "Words though the finest twine of reason, are / Too Course a web for Deity to ware." After this, the "Christographia" poems become decidedly more doctrinal, as they describe such attributes of Christ as wisdom, fullness, might, grace, truth, and power. Taylor, however, never loses sight of his own personal connection to these attributes and the hope they offer for his eventual glorification.

THE SPIRITUAL WEDDING IN THE SONG OF SONGS

Related to the hope that the idea of the Incarnation inspires in Taylor is his attention to the popular Protestant allegory that relates the songs of the bride and bridegroom in the Song of Songs, or the Book of Canticles, to the relationship of Christ to His redeemed church. Even as early as the first Meditation in Series One, Taylor employs the metaphor of the erotic relationship of a happily married bride and bridegroom to figure forth the spiritual relationship of the church or body of the faithful and Christ. Taylor often uses the imagery of physical love and marriage, traditionally based on the wedding songs in this biblical book, to express how God relates to His saints. To many Puritans, the infusion of grace into the undeserving soul at the moment of election was a kind of marriage or sexual union (Scheick 144–45). This irresistible entwining of God and the human saint also relates directly to the mystery of the Incarnation, with the intermixing of the human and divine essences that become the incarnated Christ. Exegetically, this type of erotic imagery was not only adapted from the Song of Songs but also tied to the parable of the vestal virgins and the rhetoric of love that typifies the Gospel of John. Taylor was aware of all these sources and uses many of the pertinent biblical passages in his headnotes, particularly in the Second Series.

Norman S. Grabo tries to make the case that this metaphor was particular to the Catholic mystical experience, and thus was another indication of Taylor's closet mysticism (*Taylor* 22, 46). But the Protestant exegetical tradition with which Taylor was familiar, exemplified by such works as James Durham's *Clavis Cantici: or, an Exposition of the Song of Solomon* (1668) or the various writings on the Song of Songs by Taylor's fellow Puritan John Cotton, regularly interpreted the bride of Canticles, even in the Bible's more erotic passages, as an allegory for the church or the individual saved soul being courted spiritually by the bridegroom who is Christ. Mason Lowance also discusses the relationship of this allegory to what Taylor expected life would be like after his death and glorification, a true picture of the world to come (94).

A related meditative technique that was used commonly by devotional poets in the fifteenth and sixteenth centuries was the assumption of a female persona by the male Christian poet who longed to be Christ's bride, or one of the Elect. Albert Gelpi calls this transgendered linguistic technique "an extended notion of typology," (46) and Charles Hambrick-Stowe terms it simply an erotic metaphor (17). Ivy Schweitzer notes that the male writer casting himself as a female in the face of irresistible grace helped to cure the negativity associated in Christian tradition with women because of Eve's sin (111). But the more central reason why Taylor, or any Protestant male devotional poet, would depict himself as a bride in an erotic relationship with Christ would be because the female gender seemed a more natural embodiment of the complete surrender to and dependence on the male divine principle that was part of the whole conversion process (Schweitzer 110–11). At any rate, Taylor's use of the female persona in such poems as Meditation 2.148 causes Karen Rowe to see the dominant tone of the *Preparatory Meditations* as that of a "love letter" Taylor sends to Christ (258). Taylor begins as early as Meditation 1.23, based on "Cant. 4.8. My Spouse," to place himself in a relationship of marriage with Christ, the husband who deigns to wed "backward Clay."

He ends this Meditation with the lines: "I then shall be thy Bride Espousd by thee / And thou my Bridesgroom Deare Espousde shalt bee." In later Meditations, Taylor continues to identify himself with the bride or spouse, moving away from his earlier identification with the poet David (Hammond, *Sinful Self* 225). This may indicate a transition in his own life from a concentration on himself as a writer to a focus on his own glorification.

Ivy Schweitzer has systematized the major Canticles sequence at the end of Taylor's *Preparatory Meditations* into two separate movements, both of which illuminate the marriage relationship that Taylor uses as his central metaphor (112). In her estimation, Meditations 2.115–33 focus on the bride's or spouse's praise of the bridegroom, as the Taylorian female voice rhapsodizes about the honor done to her by His attentions. Taylor variously uses the first person, in which he pictures himself as the spouse, but other times, sometimes even in the same poem, he speaks of the spouse in the third person. As the poems proceed, Taylor allegorizes and creates a conceit out of every part of the bridegroom's body, using the physical terms already provided in the Book of Canticles. Meditation 2.128 ends this technique by summing up all the bridegroom's attributes as well as his attraction to the spouse, whom Taylor (in this particular instance, not the spouse himself) asks to join with all the faithful to seek Christ. In Meditation 2.130, Taylor confidently asks the bridegroom to plant him in the garden bed of spices along with the rest of His saints. The allusion in this Meditation to the garden bed where the bridegroom can take repose on "blissfull Couches" contributes to the erotic network of images that Taylor gleans from the Song of Songs. Although the bride is not mentioned specifically in this Meditation, it is nonetheless headed with the biblical verse, "Cant. 6.2. My Beloved is gone down into his Garden, to the Beds of Spices."

Taylor's confidence appears to wane, however, in the last few Meditations that focus on the bridegroom, as he begins to express doubts that he is planted as he wishes: "Shall I no Bed of Spice, or Spices have / Rise up to entertain thee with Delight?" (Med. 2.131). He also connects these doubts characteristically to his own lack of writing skill: "And if I 'tempt to celebrate thy fame / It is too bright: my jagging pen will't stain" (Med. 2.132). But the last Meditation of this sequence based on "Cant. 6.2. I am my beloved and my beloved is mine" has Taylor declaring: "I my Beloveds am, and he my lot" and shortly after, "The Bridsgrooms all the Brids, his all is hers" (Med. 2.133). The confidence here alludes to Taylor's certainty of his election. The poem even ends with Taylor's promise to share the bridegroom who is his with the daughters of Jerusalem, and pictures all the saints and angels in heaven singing "Weddin Songs." Taylor, at that point, is secure in his conjugal relationship with his Lord.

Starting with Meditation 2.134 until 2.153, according to Schweitzer, based on Canticles 6:4 to 7:6, the focus changes to a concentration on the bride and her attributes. Taylor begins Meditation 2.134 by speaking about the bride in the third person as the "fairest of the Fairest kinde alive," the perfect saint, but gradually begins to identify with her, and then—as this sequence moves along—actually speaks in the voice of the bride in many of the later Meditations, indicating again an increased conviction of his own salvation (Davis, *Reading* 185–86; Schweitzer 123). In Meditation 2.136, Taylor creates another identity for the bride, also based on the exegetical interpretation of the Song of Songs, that of the saved church or body of the faithful: "Seeing thy Spouse that doth consist of all / Gods blesst Elect regenerate within." This identification is strengthened in the next poem, where Taylor asks to be one hair on the spouse's head, citing Canticles 6:5 as the headnote, "Thy hair is like a flock of Goats that graze on mount Gilliad." Taylor here, as in the earlier Meditation 2.130, sees himself as one of many brides, or a part of the collective bride that is the true Christian church. This identification is further solidified in Meditation 2.142, when Taylor demands forthrightly: "Make me a member of this Spouse of thine." In Meditation 2.140, he even asks for his temples to be made the color of pomegranates so that he may be like the spouse, as described in Canticles 6:7.

Meditation 2.143 marks a turning point in the sequence, as Taylor begins to realize that his demands have been met, and that he is indeed espoused to Christ. Taylor ends this poem by once again promising to sing "that Wedden Song" to Christ, or—as he puts it at the end of Meditation 2.151—the "Bridall Melodies." In Meditation 2.148, then, Taylor becomes the Prince's daughter of Canticles 7:1, whose "walk . . . in the Way of Faith / And of Repentance" qualifies him for the role. However, in the middle of this Meditation, he begins again to refer to the spouse in the third person, which sets him up to become a supplicant by the end of the poem, whose confidence appears to be waning, if only slightly.

Interestingly, almost all the poems in this sequence that precede Taylor's realization in Meditation 2.143 that he is a part of the spouse begin with an entire verse or more that apologizes for Taylor's lack of skill in writing, harking back to the dedication to art sequence in the First Series. Although the pronounced deprecation that characterizes the end of the

First Series is absent, Taylor still denigrates his skill to some extent, but offers the proviso in Meditation 2.142 that his verses will get better "[if] Thy Holy Spirit be their inward Dress." However, at the end of that Meditation, he uses the unusual image of a tennis ball to depict himself being slammed to the ground so hard that he bounces back up to heaven. From that point on, his doubts become less acute, although they are still occasionally articulated, as would be expected from a sanctified but not glorified Puritan.

When Taylor gets to the passages in Canticles that describe the bride in graphic physical detail, he becomes more consciously allegorical. In Meditation 2.149, for instance, based on "Can. 7.2. Thy Navill is a round Goblet," Taylor images the spouse as pregnant with "spirituall offspring of a spirituall race," the saintly church members, who in Meditation 2.150, with the headnote "Cant. 7.3. Thy two breasts are like two young Roes that are twins," are nursed by the new mother. In this latter Meditation, Taylor creates an analogy between the beloved's suckled breasts and the two biblical Testaments that also give nourishment—albeit spiritual rather than physical—to the infantile faithful, those that John Cotton refers to as "spiritual babes" in his 1668 sermon aimed at young people, "Spiritual Milk for Boston Babes, Drawn Out of the Breasts of Both Textaments [sic] for Their Souls Nourishment." This equation between female breasts and the two testaments of the Bible was also a commonplace in Protestant exegesis. In the Meditation, Taylor begs Christ to "put these nibbles then my mouth into / And suckle me therewith I humbly pray." Taylor then proceeds to end this sequence on the features of the bride with a poem on her neck, eyes, and nose, and another on her head and hair. The last poem that Schweitzer includes in this sequence, Meditation 2.153, has a Canticles headnote, but appears to depart from the theme of the description of the spouse and concentrates instead on Christ's own poetic ability to rhapsodize on the attractions of his spouse. Taylor finds in the poem that Christ's "Rhetorick" is an inspiration to his own writing.

Although Charles Hambrick-Stowe believes that Taylor was able to write this erotically because of his own happy marital life, Thomas Davis observes that the majority of the Canticles poems were written in Taylor's mature years. He believes that the heavy use of traditional allegory indicates that Taylor, because of his advancing age, is more interested in exploring his conviction that he actually is one of the Elect. This would explain his assumption of the bride's voice, and also make his use of the marriage metaphor a purely spiritual exercise (Hambrick-Stowe 49; Davis, *Reading* 174, 177–78). Schweitzer speculates that Taylor emphasizes the allegorical nature of the imagery because of his stereotypical Puritan prudery (95), but Hambrick-Stowe has a point: not only was Taylor happily married twice and the father of many children, but in Meditation 2.80, his unbridled joy at becoming a father again at age sixty-six emerges in the imagery of intercourse and childbirth, which he unashamedly uses as a metaphor for the infusion of grace into the Christian soul. Nor was age the only impetus for this kind of imagery. Taylor speaks of inflamed love as early as the first Meditation, and Meditation 1.35 contains allusions to the act of physical love, and its headnote is not from the Song of Songs:

> Make me the Couch on which thy Love doth ly.
> Lord make my heart thy bed, thy heart make mine.
> Thy Love bed in my heart, bed mine in thine.

When he becomes immersed in the Canticles imagery, the eroticism does become more extensive. Meditations 2.96 and 2.97 have as their headnotes "Cant. 1.2. Let him kiss me with the Kisse [Kisses] of his mouth," a biblical verse that gives Taylor license to imagine a physical relationship with Christ, even though the possibility of it being unrequited haunts him as, while he is on earth, Christ plays "bow-peep" with him. In Meditation 2.97, the spouse is not the poet, but a third person in the poem who herself begs for Christ's kisses.

PREDESTINATION AND PREPARATIONISM

The good Puritan, however, even while enraptured by the gift of Christ's Incarnation and held rapt by the possibility of being married to Christ, could never forget that these manifestations of God's ways to man had occurred to usher in the second covenant with God after humankind had foolishly squandered the first. The Puritan allegiance to covenant theology that was such an important characteristic in the establishment of the Massachusetts colonies contained an inherent contradiction that often puzzles the modern reader. Although much religious prose of the time appears to accept the assumptions intrinsic to the doctrine of Calvinist predestination while blithely insisting on Puritans' constant attention to their religious lives and practices, the many synods, heresies, and controversies that were constant features of early American life in the Puritan colonies indicate that even the best Puritans could not always balance the two. Their religious belief in predestination required each Puritan to accept as true that, due to the covenant of grace, if he or she was of the Elect, God had predetermined this before birth and nothing could change that destiny. At the same time, the philosophy of their theocracy necessitated that all Puritans who lived in the model community in New England had to be of the Elect. However, people's natural tendencies being what they are, the ministers of the colonies soon realized that if people believed God had predestined them to be saved, and especially if negative value was placed on the covenant of works, then saved Christians should not have to do anything to encourage God to do what He had already done, nor did they even need to behave like model Christians. Out of arguments to attempt to resolve this dilemma—endeavors that applied Ramist logic in order to justify the intentions behind the errand into the New England wilderness—came the doctrine of preparationism, a compromise between assurance's joy and its potential arrogance. With this doctrine, the American Puritans moved beyond the Calvinist tenet of absolutely total helplessness in the face of God's free choice of the Elect and the unregenerate, and devised a pattern by which all committed Christians in the community could ascertain at least the perception of their personal spiritual fates (Parker 159). Additionally, preparationism promoted the continuance of church membership, as established by the principles of the Cambridge Platform and the later Halfway Synod, once the complexity of the implementation of the conversion experience and its public relation compromised the growth of the theocracy.

As Andrew Delbanco defines it, preparationism is the gradual process of discovering one's own salvation (50–51). Two of the primary texts written by New England ministers that describe the process by which a soul might prepare for the infusion of grace are *The Application of Redemption* by Thomas Hooker and *The Sincere Convert* by Thomas Shepard, both reprinted many times during the seventeenth century. Both writers are interested in providing a pattern and a justification for Puritans to seek out the truth about the fate of their individual souls. Prohibited by Calvinist doctrine from convincing God that one deserved to be saved, the Puritan nevertheless desired for his or her will to be operative in the process. Even if it was meaningless to try to convince God of one's worthiness to go to heaven, at least one should be able to beseech Him to grant the gift of discernment of His intentions for the eternal life of the individual. In a subtle difference from Calvin's original theology, the Puritans in New England believed that faith had to be found before grace was infused into the regenerate soul; Calvin, on the other hand, writes that faith is a result of the infusion of grace by the Holy Spirit that becomes perceptible only through its stirrings in the human heart (Parker 142). So the original intention of preparationist doctrine was to focus the attention of the as yet unregenerate soul on sensing the infusion of grace that meant election, to ensure that each member of the Puritan congregation who was not yet saved was truly seeking that moment.

But the scope of preparationism went beyond the perception of conversion and subsequent public relation of one's conversion experience as the New England Puritan experiment continued. The lesson most saved Puritans were taught by their ministers was that even after they had experienced the act of justification, if it was genuine, the regenerate person should continue to search for more and more assurance of its legitimacy as well as to prepare for his or her subsequent glorification. The middle stage, the one that most looks like a person trying to influence God to take him or her to heaven by allegiance to the covenant of works, is sanctification. This term refers to the time of life when one tries to be as perfect a Christian as possible, motivated by love of God and desire for the Christian appearance of one's community (Hambrick-Stowe 10). Many sixteenth- and seventeenth-century Protestant guides to faith thus focus both on the importance of preparing to encounter the moment of justification, and then keeping on the same path that led to this positive discernment of one's spiritual fate. If one looks at the *Preparatory Meditations* as such a spiritual journey, then most of the spiritual work that is chronicled in that collection occurs after the initial conversion experience that Taylor describes in the fourth poem.

In his account of Puritan theology, *Visible Saints*, Edmund Morgan cites the British Puritan William Perkins as one major proponent of preparationism. Of the ten steps Perkins delineates that would lead a person to realization of his or her own helplessness in the face of irresistible grace, the first four are preparatory (68–69). Thus, even though Puritan Calvinist doctrine stipulated that an individual could do nothing about his own salvation, preparationism allowed the illusion that man could at least find out, if not influence God, about his or her eventual spiritual fate (Keller, "Taylor" 193). This illusion, in order to maintain its balance with the doctrine of predestination, became quite ambiguous, so that the Puritan could behave well and attend to such ordinances as prayer, meditation, and listening to sermons in order to prepare for the moment of conversion (although he could not invite that moment) and, after he was a convinced

saint, he could still continue to prepare for his glorification by anticipating, and actually living as much as possible in the anticipation, of what
heaven would be like. As John Gatta says, and Taylor does, the preparing
Puritan could also seek to relive the ultimate moment of the conversion
experience (84, 91). Additionally, the gradualness of the process kept the
individual in a prayerful and meditative mode, which thus cemented the
appearance and reputation of the Puritan communities in the eyes of
the Christian world.

By the time Taylor began writing his meditative poetry, the "city on
the hill" that John Winthrop had theorized in 1630 had become a reality,
although a considerably more hard-won reality than Winthrop had imag-
ined. Westfield was just one of several congregations trying to appear as
perfect Christian communities in the eyes of the world, most particularly
in the eyes of the faithful left in England. As such, the magistrates and
ministers of the congregational communities realized that the members
could not just bask in their own sainthood, but that they needed to work
constantly to prove to the world (and themselves) that they were the
model Christians that they said they were. Thus, the individual search
for salvation became a community project meant to foreground the sainthood of all whom God had chosen.[2] Because of this influence in his
society, Taylor's voice in the meditative poetry as a whole appears to
demonstrate preparationism at its best (Keller, "Taylor" 190–91). Karl
Keller indeed sees Taylor's self-deprecation about both his poetry and his
spiritual state as part of such a performance of prepared worthiness ("Taylor" 193). As the Puritan years wore on, as William Scheick points out,
it even became considered sinful or a mark of deception if an elect Puritan
was not preparing the way for the entry of God's grace (or the discovery
of the entry of God's grace, or his or her glorified entrance into heaven)
(87–88).

The voice of the *Preparatory Meditations*, then, is the preparing soul.
Keller suggests that the reason Taylor felt it was unnecessary to publish
his poems was just because they were part of his personal search for evidence of his own salvation (*Example* 93). That Taylor revised, ordered,
and bound them neatly, however, suggests that his individual grasp of the
need to prepare for the potential entry of God's grace was as much meant
for a community—even a future community—as for Taylor himself. Reading the poems over three hundred years later, the twenty-first-century
reader can identify with the quest for a relationship to Christ much more
than he or she could relate to what might have been a pompous assurance
that only Puritans could get to heaven.

PROTESTANT MEDITATION

One of the ordinances that was often prescribed by ministers and writers of religious treatises as a positive way to prepare for the infusion of grace or for eternal life in heaven was meditation. Much scholarship has examined the meditative techniques that were known to the New England Puritans and that inspired Edward Taylor to write such a large body of meditative poetry, beginning with the 1954 landmark book *The Poetry of Meditation: A Study in English Religious Literature* by Louis Martz. In it, Martz defines a poet's "meditative style" as "[an expression of] the unique being of an individual who has learned, by intense mental discipline, to live his life in the presence of divinity" (324). That surely qualifies Taylor to be a meditative poet in the league of the others whom Martz includes in his study, such as John Donne, Robert Southwell, and George Herbert. Early Taylor scholarship attempted to find roots for Taylor's meditative practices in medieval writing on meditation by such Roman Catholic clerics as St. Bernard, St. Ignatius, and St. Francis de Sales, all of whom Martz discusses in detail. Finding his impetus in Taylor's prose, Norman S. Grabo uses Taylor's adaptation of common seventeenth-century meditative techniques as still another way to ally him with medieval mysticism, seeing his insistence on the *imitatio Christi* in the *Christographia* sermons to be similar to the medieval mystic's quest for perfect unity with God (*Taylor* 50). Furthermore, Grabo cites Taylor's use of such words as "rapt" and "rapture" and his occasional linguistic creation of a visual picture—such as the tree of life in Meditation 1.29—as modeled after classic Catholic mystical techniques (*Taylor* 40–41). Grabo even states that Taylor's raptures would probably cause him to fall into a trance and perhaps actually experience separation of the soul from the body as it joined with Christ (*Taylor* 22). He also pictures the writing of the *Preparatory Meditations* as Taylor's retreat from the Puritan world altogether into his own private, quasi-mystical, closet Catholic environment (*Taylor* 80).

But such characterizations of Taylor as a unique or closet Puritan mystic seem to relate to a misunderstanding or lack of knowledge about the actual process of Puritan meditative practices, both its similarities to and differences from the earlier Catholic tradition (Scheick 152). They were not essentially identical. The medieval mystic participated in unions with the divine while on earth, moments of bliss when all sense of self was lost and the individual experienced perfect absorption in Christ. Taylor's poetry throughout, and more so toward the end of the Second Series of the *Preparatory Meditations*, offers a belief that perfect union with God is only possible after death. Even in his more joyful and optimistic poems, and even in light of the mystery of the Incarnation, Taylor never seems to lose sight of the perpetually sorry condition of the soul while it is locked in the body on earth.

Martz himself delineates differences between the Catholic, the Protestant, and the specifically Puritan practices of meditation, citing the chief meditative manual for seventeenth-century Puritans as Richard Baxter's *The Saints Everlasting Rest* (1650). More recent scholarship examines Protestant meditative practices in England and New England, set forth first by such British devotional writers as Baxter and earlier by Joseph Hall in his *The Art of Divine Meditation* (1607). These Protestant writers agree with their Catholic forebears in the description of a three-part process for the meditator, the first being the central examination of one's own spiritual state, described by Baxter in more Protestant terms of preaching to oneself. This would be followed by analysis of the state through the creation of a mental picture of Christ's life or, more pertinent to the Protestant, contemplation of His divine attributes and doctrines, always inspired by the words of scripture. The third stage then would be the consequent stirring up of the affections toward performing one's Christian duty, something that could be properly done on earth to help the Christian lead a better life in this world, or—more pertinent to Puritan meditation—toward ascertaining one's spiritual fate.

But real differences existed in the way that Protestants, and even more so Puritans, adapted meditative techniques from the work of the Catholics who were heretics to them. Martz discusses how the Puritan belief in irresistible and nonmerited grace complicates the motivation for meditation (156–57). To make meditation a useful activity to those whose election was assured, Baxter and others have to resort to the value of preparationism, tying Protestant meditation to activity meant to solidify the reputation of the Protestant or Puritan community, as well as a necessary and constant attention to the words of scripture rather than to the vagaries of one's own imagination, even a Christ-centered creative faculty. One impetus for Grabo and others to theorize that Taylor might be a mystic is his constant attention to the Book of Canticles, or the Song of Songs, as a vehicle for his meditative composition of place. However, Taylor's use of this Old Testament book rests on his strong belief in its allegorical nature and the ubiquitous Protestant exegetical technique of Christologizing the love story of Solomon and his Bride to foreshadow or serve as a type of the marriage of Christ's divine nature with the human nature of his faithful, another source for Taylor's favorite theme. Ivy

Schweitzer points out that this allegorical reading of Canticles is markedly Protestant in nature (113). Additionally, Ursula Brumm notes that some distinct differences exist in Catholic meditative practices that focus on the emotion and passion of the life and suffering of Christ and Protestant practices that use words from scripture as their vehicle (Brumm, "Meditative" 318–19; Keller, *Example* 92; Hambrick-Stowe 18). Richard Baxter does emphasize that the analysis stage should be practiced on doctrinal statements and involve the discursive understanding that could plumb the significance of the scriptural language, rather than creating fancy visual images or emotional rhapsodies from such contemplation (Martz 160, Eberwein 66). John Gatta, in his study of Taylor's comic spirit, also notes that his meditative wit—like that of the typical Protestant meditator—is anchored in language, specifically the "intertextuality" of scripture (50–51).

Of course, the ur text for the inspiration and content of these meditative practices was itself linguistic and part of the Bible, and one that has already been identified as a major influence on Taylor. The Book of Psalms became the Protestant and Puritan model for meditative practices, based on early Christian tradition, and its author David became, along with his other identifications in Protestant exegesis, the model Christian meditator. The traditional three stages of Protestant meditation are all found in the Psalms. The tripartite structure that can be identified in many of the *Preparatory Meditations* clearly echoes this traditional structure.

Puritan meditation was also connected intrinsically to the sacrament of the eucharist. Because of the relatively small number of ordinances present in Puritan worship, one predominant focus of meditation was searching one's soul for the evidence of conversion necessary for legitimate reception of the Lord's Supper (Brumm, "Meditative" 32). This connection between meditation and the eucharist is made most evident by the title of Taylor's collection. One source he may have consulted for this belief was the *Shorter Catechism* of the Westminster Assembly, composed in 1648 and followed by many Puritans, which tied meditation to a person's ability to receive the Supper faithfully (Grabo, *Taylor* 35–36).

The Book of Psalms also factored into this connection in a major way. Psalms were traditionally sung during communion services and recommended by Puritan preachers as private meditations before the Supper. They were clearly identified with the preparation needed before participation at the Supper; David's soliloquizing, for example, had been recognized as early as the writings of John Calvin as an example of the proper mode of meditative self-examination. Furthermore, a number of Psalms were identified in Christologizing Protestant exegesis as eucharistical hymns, in which David is pictured as longing for the sacrament. Psalm 63 is an example, in which David's pronouncement that "My soul shall be satisfied as with marrow and fatness; / And my mouth shall praise thee with joyful lips"[3] appears to link his appreciation for God's gift of the eucharist with the impetus to offer meditative praise. David thus becomes in this way an obvious model for what Taylor is attempting to do in the *Preparatory Meditations*.

Furthermore, the belief in the use of imagery—written or visual—as a vehicle for raising the meditative affections also has an effect on how Taylor uses nature imagery in his poetry. Jeffrey Hammond notes that Taylor is only interested in nature as long as it relates to God's creative power or the negative carnality of human nature (*Sinful Self* 166); William J. Scheick observes that the only nature imagery or ideas acceptable to Taylor were those found in scripture (137). Nature as a source of imagery in any modern or Romantic sense would, of course, appear to a Puritan as a Satan-inspired trap (Scheick 4). Nevertheless, one effect of the close self-examination that was characteristic of Puritan spiritual life was a belief in an analogic view of reality, which saw many natural occurrences, even ones that seemed to be trivial, as signs of spiritual truth (Keller, *Example* 57–58). For example, Taylor uses numerous images and allusions to the natural medicine of his day as vehicles for explaining the work of Christ on the prepared soul, as in Meditation 1.4, where he pictures many uses of the rose that were in current medical practice, and allegorizes them as the workings of Christ, or the Rose of Sharon, on the souls of saved Christians:

> The Rosy Oyle, from Sharons Rose extract
>   Better than Palma Christi far is found.
> Its Gilliads Balm for Conscience when she's wrackt
>   Unguent Apostolorum for each Wound.
>   Let me thy Patient, thou my Surgeon bee.
>   Lord, with thy Oyle of Roses Supple mee.

Taylor's allusions to such contemporary remedies as palma Christi, another name for castor oil, and the balm of Gilead, or Mecca balsam, display the knowledge of a physician. At the same time, as Donald Stanford indicates in his note to this poem, Taylor was also aware of the imagistic commonplace that Christ's blood could be like medicine to the suffering soul (Taylor, *Poems* 12). Taylor thus allegorizes nature, but also displays his own familiarity with the human uses of nature. In fact, one reason Grabo offers to reject Taylor as a mystic is that he doesn't always see nature as necessarily sacramental, as many medieval mystics do (*Taylor* 92).

A characteristic example of how Taylor uses nature as a meditative vehicle is the occasional poem "Upon a Wasp Child with Cold." His composition of the picture of a wasp using the sun to warm its stiffened body prompts him to surmise the instinctive knowledge the wasp has—which to the human Taylor seems like rational thought—that the sun is its "Apothecaries Shop." Taylor then moves from what might have been a mere anthropomorphizing of an insect to a view of the wasp as a "school and a schoolmaster" who teaches Taylor to both work toward salvation and trust in the power of the Son. Again, as in Meditation 1.4, the natural observation becomes a sign of a spiritual truth of use to the Puritan.

In the valedictory poems, however, Taylor appears to reject altogether this habit of meditation on the creatures, even though it was one form of contemplation espoused by such Protestant devotional writers as John Calvin, Thomas Taylor, John Preston, and Richard Baxter. In this poem, Taylor voices a lack of trust in the cosmos because of its transience, and scorns carnal man for being too bound to earth. Although he later states that he has appreciated the use of carnal items as stepping stones to glory, he is not averse to leaving them behind. This rejection may be specifically related to Taylor's closeness to his own death and relative assurance of his imminent glorification at the time he is writing this poem.

Nature imagery, however, is only one small part of the number of meditative techniques that inform devotional writing in the seventeenth century. Taylor clearly responds in his poetry to the Protestant differences in meditation, such as the allegiance to logic and language over mystical emotions, and reliance, as always, on the Bible and biblical exegesis for his principles and techniques.

NOTES

1. Gatta finds Taylor's enthusiasm in these early poems to revel in the "comic incongruity" of the joining of the human and divine (21–22).

2. Edmund Morgan attributes the roots of this practice to Augustine's theory of two churches of saints, one invisible and one visible. The visible church, that which existed on earth, contained all those people whom God had elected, some of whom knew they were elected and some of whom did not. The goal of most Puritan congregations, then, was to make the visible church as close to the invisible church as humanly possible (3).

3. Biblical quotes in this book are from the King James Version.

6 Poetic Art

Taylor's imagery and prosody are largely biblically based, with special attention to the images, points of view, literary figures, and Hebrew prosodic elements found in the Book of Psalms. Nevertheless, the entire Bible was a model for Taylor, a source of language that was still human but that God had sanctioned for human writers to use.

IMAGERY

Many of Taylor's major image clusters, particularly those found in the *Preparatory Meditations*, come from the Bible, many more from Taylor's consideration of various exegetical metaphors that had been adapted from biblical words, as well as other art forms that had been modeled on the Bible, such as emblem books. Some of the imagery or particular use of the imagery, however, is purely Taylor.

Taylor's propensity for the use of the metaphysical conceit and apparent playful love of the English language itself often allows his poetry to disintegrate in the face of intriguing puzzles or wordplays. The first verse of Meditation 2.17, for example, makes Taylor's use of repetition seem more of a tongue twister than anything else:

> Thou Great Supream, thou Infinite first One:
>   Thy Being Being gave to all that be
> Yea to the best of Beings thee alone
>   To serve with Service best for best of fee.

But man the best servd thee the Worst of all
And so the Worst of incomes on him falls.

Thomas Davis writes also of the interlocking and doubling of rhyme in the dedication to art sequence at the end of the First Series, which he attributes to Taylor's desire to showcase the theme of singing (*Reading* 90). Perhaps one of Taylor's major weaknesses is to let his love of the sound and lexical flexibility of English get the best of him.

Many of Taylor's major images and image clusters come from the Book of Canticles, the text on which his first meditative poem is imagistically based and the one that Taylor turns to at the end of his life and poetic career. But other categories of imagery recur throughout his poetry that come from other biblical sources, from Christian iconography, and sometimes only from the power of his own imagination.

One of his favorite image clusters revolves around the scriptural picture of the garden, both the Garden of Eden and also the setting of the action in Canticles. Before Taylor begins his extended sequence on the Song of Songs in the Second Series, he starts and then stops two smaller sequences with headnotes from this biblical book that focus specifically on the image of the garden.

Starting with Meditation 2.63 through 2.65, Taylor creates an image cluster around the "garden of nuts" in Canticles 6:11, which he sees as an allegory for the church. He also compares this Canticles garden to the hanging gardens of Babylon, but establishes its quintessential parallel as the Garden of Eden before the fall of man. The nuts themselves are allegorized in Meditation 2.63 as "Spirituall Food, and Physike." At the end of each garden poem in this sequence, Taylor also pictures himself as a fruit or plant in the garden, or the garden bed itself. Taylor revisits the nut garden later in Meditation 2.144, using identical imagery and theme, providing unintentional humor to a modern audience by referring to Christ's church as "thy Nutty Garden."

Meditation 2.83 starts the second garden sequence, using "Can. 5.1. I am come into my Garden, etc." as the headnote. This meditation begins with a picture of the Garden of Eden, but the first verse ends with the second garden, a "Garden-Church" that, in the latter verses, becomes the Garden-Soul of the characteristic redeemed Christian. Meditations 2.84–86 stay with this verse from Canticles, repeating and embroidering the same allegorical image. Meditation 2.85 ends with a plea to Christ to be Taylor's gardener.

After the Canticles sequence at the end of the Second Series begins in earnest, Meditation 2.129 returns to the garden image, which is now

cast as the garden of the beloved that was designed by Christ, an image
that Taylor employs in the next few Meditations as he begins to focus on
the bride and bridegroom imagery in Canticles. But the garden imagery
starts as early as Meditation 1.5, also based on a passage from Canticles,
where Taylor expresses the wish, "Oh! that my Soul thy Garden were."
Meditations 2.129 through 2.132 continue to focus on the garden image,
which Taylor uses here as a metaphor for heaven, and depicts as redolent
with pleasant spices, echoing the headnote for Meditation 2.130: "Cant.
6.2. My Beloved is gone down into his Garden, to the Beds of Spices."
An alternate version of the garden is the "Pasture" that Taylor alludes to
in Meditation 1.45, where he pleads with God to be His pasture "Where
thy choice Flowers, and Hearbs of Grace shine trim."

The dichotomy of the well-tended and planted garden or pasture and
the wilderness outside it, which Taylor alludes to several times in his
poetry, adds a unique American Puritan complexity to this image. This
contrast appears in the Bible, but was more pertinently resonant in the
Puritans' real life. The wilderness/garden opposition is actually used in
the text of the Cambridge Platform of 1648, which delineated some of
the earliest rules followed in the New England Puritan theocracy, as well
as in the texts of countless other Puritan sermons and religious treatises.[1]
Taylor employs this variation of the garden image as he pictures his own
soul as a garden taken over by the wilderness in Meditation 2.4, and begs
Christ to "Fatten my Soile, and prune / My Stock," turning the weed-
infested wildness of his soul into a garden. In Meditation 2.10, he also
uses the biblical story of Moses' farewell to the wilderness as a type for
the wish of the redeemed soul to be removed from that untamed (or in
his parlance, ungraced) state.

Several other images we see particularly in the *Preparatory Meditations*
relate to this Canticles-inspired image of the garden—the pomegranate,
ointment, the Rose of Sharon, and the lily of the valley are all images
that come from this biblical book (Lewalski 418). Meditation 1.4 is based
on "Cant. 2.1. I am the Rose of Sharon" and allows Taylor to use some
of his medical knowledge to create a conceit that has the flower distilled
to produce spiritual cures for the "Consumptive Souls." The next numbered Meditation has as its headnote "Cant. 2.1. The Lilly of the Vallies"
and asks Christ to be Taylor's lily. Meditation 2.160 uses this same verse
from the Song of Songs to create a poem at the end of Taylor's poetic
career with the same plea to Christ to be Taylor's lily and become planted
in the garden of his soul.

A related image Taylor uses, common in Christian iconography, is the
tree of life or the Jesse tree. A familiar figure in emblem books and Chris-

tian iconography, the Jesse tree is based on a passage from Isaiah 11 and is meant to illustrate the genealogical lineage of Christ's human nature. Most emblems depict Jesse, the father of the psalmist David, lying on a bed or couch with the tree growing out of his body. Old Testament personages hang from the branches of the tree, with Christ and Mary His mother and sometimes a variety of angels at the top of the tree. The tree of life has other guises as well, such as the "golden tree" in the Garden of Eden that forms the central metaphor in Meditation 1.29, which Taylor declares is his "Deare-Deare Lord." In this poem, he also asks that his own "Withred Twig" be grafted onto that tree, an interesting metaphor for his hope for salvation. In Meditation 2.33 he ties this image to his favorite theme of the Incarnation by specifically saying that the tree of life, which is Christ, is related to "Theanthropie." Perhaps the quintessential verse about Christ as the tree of life appears in Meditation 2.56:

> Thou art a Tree of Perfect nature trim
>   Whose golden lining is of perfect Grace
> Perfum'de with Deity unto the brim,
>   Whose fruits, of the perfection, grow, of Grace.
>   Thy Buds, thy Blossoms, and thy fruits adorne
>   Thyselfe, and Works, more shining than the morn.

Taylor also uses the apple tree from Canticles 2:3, there a simile for the beloved, to image Christ in Meditations 2.161A and 2.161B. In these poems, which appear actually to be two versions of the same poem, the Christ-tree bears golden apples, and the poet contrasts it with the tree of the knowledge of good and evil in the Garden of Eden. In a related image from Meditation 2.33, he pictures the eucharist as an apple that drops in man's mouth from the tree that is Christ. Besides feeding Taylor with its fruit, other tree images allow him to bask in their shade and be revived by their aroma.

Another common image cluster that Taylor uses throughout the *Preparatory Meditations* consists of images of containment. Albert Gelpi identifies this imagery of boxes, cabinets, and containers as part of the erotic image cluster that emerges from his familiarity with the allegory of the bride and bridegroom of Canticles (37–38). Sometimes the image of the box is doctrinal, as in Meditation 2.50, where Taylor's image alludes to Pandora's box that breaks and releases all sin into the world. But what he presents here is a box in the Garden of Eden, crafted by God and containing all truth. In the second verse of the poem, Taylor parallels the box with the human body, most likely that of Eve, and its capacity for procreation:

> Which Box should forth a race of boxes send
>   Teemd from its Womb such as itselfe, to run
> Down from the Worlds beginning to its end.
>   But, o! this box of Pearle Fell, Broke, undone.

Although Taylor most often does use the human body as the tenor for this metaphor of the cabinet or box, the human sexual act, which he relates to opening the cabinet, is used as a metaphor for the spiritual act of the infusion of grace. In several poems, Taylor creates a situation where he is locked up and Christ has the key or, as in Meditation 1.49, is invited to pick the lock. In Meditation 1.25, for example, Taylor complains that he cannot "unscrew Loves Cabbinet" and give the Lord his heart. He returns to this image in Meditation 1.42, where his door appears rusty and the lock needs the oil of Christ's grace, and later he asks Christ also to unlock his own wardrobe and take out the wedding garment for Taylor to wear. The parallel to the erotic relationship Taylor posits in other poems is evidenced in such passages as: "O pick't [the lock]: and through the key-hole make thy way / And enter in: and let thy joyes run o're" (Med. 1.49). Alternately, in Meditation 2.115, Taylor asks God to lock up his box with the key of the scripture. As this poem focuses on the love relationship between the spouse and Christ, the allusion to a biblical chastity belt cannot be ignored.

Less often, Christ Himself is the cabinet, as in Meditation 2.46 where Christ's human body is a "Cabbinet" set with "transcendent Stones." Also in Meditation 2.50, cited above, the Pandora's box that contains evil is replaced by a "Choice pearle-made-Box," like the first one containing all truth, but this time an allegory for Christ's human body. This poem ends with Taylor's appropriate promise to "embox [Christ] in [his] heart." In Meditation 2.53, it is God's heart that is the box and Christ who has the key to unlock it. Still, the intimation of erotic activity is present as Taylor uses this metaphor for the desired relationship between himself and Christ.

Because Taylor's meditative poems were written with the Lord's Supper in mind, one cannot help but notice the many images he uses that relate exegetically to sacramental themes and spring from biblical passages that deal either directly or indirectly, through their use by Protestant exegetes, with the eucharist.

Clothing imagery abounds in Taylor's verse, with the two general positive categories being royal robes and the "wedden garment" whose absence causes the wedding guest in Christ's parable from Matthew 22:1–14 to be cast out of the festivities into the darkness that is an allegory for hell. Karen Rowe observes that Taylor uses this image particularly in those poems that were written at the time period when he was most involved with refuting Solomon Stoddard's opening of the sacrament to the unconverted (163, 206–7). Indeed, the metaphors of the wedding garment and the feast that can only be attended if the garment is worn are the focus of the entire sermon collection, the *Treatise concerning the Lord's Supper*, that Taylor wrote in 1693 in response to Stoddard's actions, and in which Taylor defines the wedding garment as "the robe of evangelical righteousness" or the proof of one's conversion (xiii). Thomas Davis finds Taylor's use of the wedding garment image to be far more ubiquitous than just in the anti-Stoddard poems, however (*Reading* 30).

Although Norman Grabo observes in his introduction to the *Treatise concerning the Lord's Supper* that Taylor came from a textile center in England and thus might have had life experience that influenced him to use the metaphor of weaving and clothing, Taylor's clothing metaphors are clearly based on biblical imagery (xi). Taylor depicts himself as the parable's wedding guest in Meditation 2.62, where angels stare at him because he attempts to approach the feast wearing rags. Rowe suggests that Taylor views his own poetry as potential wedding garments that will replace the rags and facilitate his own entry into heaven (221–22). Meditation 2.56 bears this speculation out, with Taylor asking Christ to weave for him "A Damask Web of Velvet Verse" that he can use to describe Christ more correctly. Also, in Meditation 2.164, Taylor writes:

> But, oh Dear Lord, though my pen pikes no gold
>   To lace these robes with, I would dress thee in
> And its a Shame that Tinsyl ribbon should
>   Be all the trimming that I own to bring.

Here, Taylor makes a garment for Christ to wear out of the ink with which he writes. In the fourth sermon contained in the *Treatise concerning the Lord's Supper*, Taylor focuses on the speechlessness that grips the improperly clothed wedding guest in Christ's parable, further reinforcing Taylor's mental connection of the lack of the proper wedding garment and the inability to generate sufficient praise of Christ.

Throughout the meditative poetry, Taylor also describes glorious robes either worn by Christ or brought out of the grave by Him for Taylor to wear. Variously, the clothes that Christ makes for His beloved are white, to signify their purity, or red, to stand for the sacrifice of His human body that made regeneracy possible. Taylor is perhaps best known for one poem that fashions this image into a sustained conceit, the occasional poem "Huswifery." In it, Taylor images himself as the spinning wheel and the loom that will potentially produce the holy robes that, in the last two lines of the poem, Taylor puts on: "Then mine apparell shall display before yee / That I am Cloathd in Holy robes for glory." Also in Meditation 1.46, based on the headnote "Rev. 3.5. The same shall be cloathed in White Raiment," Taylor again uses the image of the loom, this time a "Loom Divine" whereon Christ has spun the "whitest Lawn" with which to make clothes for those who belong to Him. The regenerate spouse of the Book of Canticles also wears white clothing "of Spirituall Silk / Of th'Web wove in the Heavens bright Loom" (Med. 2.143).

One of the most interesting uses of clothing imagery stems from Taylor's fascination with the Incarnation:

> My Deare-Deare Lord, my Heart is Lodgd in thee:
>   Thy Person lodgd in bright Divinity
> And waring Cloaths made of the best web bee
>   Wove in the golde Loom of Humanity.
>   All lin'de and overlaide with Wealthi'st lace
>   The finest Silke of Sanctifying Grace. (Med. 2.128)

Here, Taylor combines both the simpler, though expensive, clothes of humanity with the fancier overlay of divinity that marks the hypostatic union.

Taylor also often uses the biblical image of a banquet table prepared for a feast that clearly is a metaphor for the Lord's Supper, which in various poems takes place both on earth and in heaven. As early as "The Reflexion" in the First Series, Taylor pictures Christ at the head of a table and expresses his doubts as to whether he has been invited to the feast. Taylor's scriptural sources for the banquet include Isaiah 25:6, the feast of fat things, which Taylor uses as a headnote to Meditation 1.11; the allusion to the feast in 1 Corinthians 5:8, which serves as the headnote to Meditation 2.71; and even Revelations 3:10: "He that over comes will I give to eat of the Hidden Mannah," which becomes a banquet image that controls the development of Meditation 2.159. In Meditation 2.110, Taylor makes his own connection to the feast clear: "And this rich banquet makes me thus a Poet."

Like the wedding garment image cluster, the feast becomes a dominant image in poems inspired by the Stoddard controversy. Meditation 2.108, for example, based on the headnote "Matt. 26.26.27. Jesus took bread—and he took the Cup," pictures a royal feast where all present are wearing robes made by Christ. Taylor brings up the feast image later in Meditation 2.156, which begins a short subsequence within the Canticles sequence on "Cant. 5.1. Eate oh Friendes and drink yea drink abundantly oh Beloved" and "Cant. 2.4. He brought me into the Banqueting house and his banner over me was Love." Here, Taylor interprets these images as his invitation to "thy Rich Garden feast" (Med. 2.156).

Meditations 8–11 in the First Series are particularly full of sacramental food and drink images, with their thematic emphasis on the Lord's Supper. Many of these are embroidered by Taylor through the power of the poetic conceit. The communion bread becomes associated with the bread of life, and the communion altar becomes the biblical feast. The communion wine also becomes intertwined with aqua vitae, or the water of life. In fact, all of Taylor's food and drink imagery relates to the sacramental emphasis of his poetry, as the food is most often bread or manna and the drink is water of life or wine. In Meditation 2.86, additionally, a feast in the Canticles garden features bread, wine, milk, and honey. Ursula Brumm suggests a connection between Taylor's use of such food imagery and the process of meditation, because in that devotional method ideas about God are mentally chewed and digested ("Meditative" 330). Taylor bears out this association in Meditation 2.138, referring to the teeth of the spouse in the Book of Canticles: "Teeth are for the eating of the Food made good / And Meditation Chawing is the Cud," a theme he explores for the rest of the poem. Grabo sees him as muddying his imagery with this kind of "kitchen details," finding the domestic bent in Taylor's imagery to be indecorous (*Taylor* 95). But Lewalski sees the food and drink imagery as a way of emphasizing the antithetical breach between God and Taylor, citing particularly the kitchen metaphors he uses to image communion in Meditation 1.8 (401).

Part of Taylor's idiosyncratic appeal is based in his use of such domestic and homespun metaphors, which create a jarring effect when juxtaposed to the more familiar biblically based imagery (Rowe 246). Although some critics have pointed out that Taylor's existence on the frontier might have made the imagery of domesticity and the rustic a commonplace reaction to his environment or even a characteristic Americanness about his writing (Keller, *Example* 59, 165), others see this usage as much as the decorous biblical imaging as spiritually based, a devotional writer's habit that itself is an outgrowth of attention to the words of the Bible or a consideration of his own meek status in relationship to the glory of Christ. Richard Daly sees Taylor's frequent use of a humble stance as a way for him to avoid unchristian pride in his own work (196). William Scheick sees Taylor's homely imagery as an offering of himself to God as someone who needs to be refined (130). However, as indicated earlier, the domestic imagery found in such poems as Meditation 1.8 is actually used to picture God Himself as the baker, a technique called domestication of the infinite, perhaps meant to underscore Taylor's affection for the mystery of the Incarnation and his belief that indeed it changed the antithetical relationship between the human and the divine to one of, if not equality, at least closeness and sharing (Grabo, *Taylor* 65). This view of God, furthermore, can be related to the depiction of the merciful, loving, even motherly Christ whom Taylor gives voice to in several poems in *Gods Determinations*.

The kitchen seems to be a favorite setting for Taylor's domestic imagery, which would relate to his focus on the food of the Lord's Supper. Besides depicting God as a baker, Christ becomes a cook and even a restauranteur, and the angels—dressed in white—become waiters. In several Meditations in the Second Series, he also pictures heaven as a bakery, and in Meditation 1.31, he figures forth Satan as a cook who sauces every dish with sin.

Taylor's domestic imagery is often coupled in discussion with his use of self-deprecation, his often sadomasochistic groveling before his Lord and his employment of the imagery of scatology and disease. Many critics have pointed out that the use of self-deprecation is a time-honored technique of meditative and devotional poets. John Gatta has even suggested that the way Taylor employs the technique goes beyond traditional ritual to parody (21). Most critics, however, view Taylor's denigration of his own spiritual state and writing ability as sincere. Thomas Davis ties the increased vehemence in the poems written between 1688 and 1692 to outside events in his life, such as his growing concern with the way in which Stoddard had begun to erode the orthodox ground on which the Puritan sacraments stood and, more personally, the death of his sixth daughter Hezekiah, which occurred as he penned the poems at the end of Series One (*Reading* 99; Grabo, *Taylor* 30). At any rate, the self-deprecation in the First Series begins rather gently as, for example, in Meditation 1.22 with allusions to his "Hide bound Soule" and declarations such as: "My Quaintest Metaphors are ragged Stuff, / Making the Sun seem like a Mullipuff," and then in the next Meditation, with references to "my

Rough Voice" and "my blunt Tongue." This deprecation, particularly in relation to Taylor's own writing, becomes more and more intense throughout the remainder of the First Series, with references to himself in Meditation 1.25 as "starke nakt, rowld all in mire, undone," a decidedly violent depiction with sexual undertones. In Meditation 1.36, he contrasts Christ's kindness with his own vileness caused by the overwhelmingly evil nature of his sin, and by Meditation 1.40, he is calling himself:

> A Sty of Filth, a Trough of Washing-Swill
>   A Dunghill Pit, a Puddle of mere Slime.
>   A Nest of Vipers, Hive of Hornets; Stings.
>   A Bag of Poyson, Civit-Box of Sins.

In Meditation 1.45, he ties the deprecation specifically to his carnal passions: "My Members Dung-Carts that bedung at pleasure, / My Life, the Pasture where Hells Hurdloms leasure." Although the concentration of this negativity is in the final poems of the First Series, even as late as 1698, in Meditation 2.26, Taylor refers to himself as "A bag of botches, Lump of Loathsomeness: / Defild by Touch, by Issue: Leproust flesh." He refers again to his leprosy in the following Meditation, tying it to his carnal existence. This use of such a disease metaphor for sin actually occurs often in the *Meditations*, and in Meditations 2.67[B] and 2.69, Taylor's medical vocation becomes apparent as he accumulates a list of diseases and "Spirituall Maladies" that can only be cured by Christ's "Surgeons Shop" where He busily makes "Cordiall powders," mustard plaster, and a "Rheum-Cap," among other potions and medical remedies, to cure all of Taylor's foul diseases.

Another common image cluster found in the *Preparatory Meditations* consists of a variety of physical transporting devices—conduits and pipes, ladders and chutes. Almost always, the pipes are in heaven and either God, Christ, or the angels use them to send messages, or more often, floods of grace down to man on earth. Meditation 1.10, for example, first depicts "Aqua-Vitae" running down from "Heav'ns high Hill" to allay the poet's thirst, but in the next verse, the water is being conveyed by "Golden Pipes" that are Christ's veins, made human by the mystery of the Incarnation, and then opened by the scourging and beating that led to His death and the redemptive act. In Meditation 2.60[B], the aqua vitae gushes out of the wound on Christ's side for Taylor to drink. As this poem builds imagery of richness, the liquid becomes liquor and wine, an allusion to the wedding feast of Cana where Christ also changed water to wine, which is itself used in exegesis as an allusion to the eucharist. In Meditation 2.121, the "golden Streams" made out of "Gospell Doctrine" run out of Christ's mouth and land on Taylor's heart. In the later Canticles sequence, Meditation 2.142 depicts the spouse as being the recipient of Christ's love, that comes "tumbling on her" from "golden pipes that spout / In Streams from heaven."

William J. Scheick has also connected the image of these conduit pipes to the musical "pipe" that Taylor cites often in relation to his need to praise God and contribute to Him the gift of poetry (126–27). Indeed, in Meditation 1.22, Taylor begs of Christ: "That I thy glorious Praise may Trumpet right, / Be thou my Song, and make Lord, mee thy Pipe." This wish is countered in Meditation 2.23 by Taylor's admission that his pipe is a "poor Creaking Pipe" and in Meditation 2.44 that it is an "Oaten Straw." Here, the conduit image reverses itself, with the motion going up from Taylor to heaven. Also, in Meditation 2.126, Taylor turns from a contemplation of Christ's windpipe, based on Canticles 5:16, that describes the Bridegroom's mouth, palate, and windpipe, to a plea to "make my Winde Pipe thy sweet praises sing." Albert Gelpi has suggested that these conduit images also share in the erotic complex of imagery that Taylor employs, allying them with the marriage allegory that is so central to his verse (41).

The pipe is, of course, one of several musical images that Taylor uses throughout his poetry. His own mental connection to the Old Testament poet David, whose harp playing was so instrumental to the success of the Hebrews, and his use of the Book of Psalms and the traditions of psalmody that were so central in the Puritan culture, make the connection between poetry and music a natural one. Ivy Schweitzer notes that over two-thirds of the Meditations use imagery of musical instruments, often with Christ as the musician (84), but just as often Taylor. He refers variously to trumpets, harps (even David's harp from the Old Testament), bells, virginals, organs, and violins as positive instruments on which to raise praises to Christ. In Meditation 2.51, he cites bagpipes as more difficult instruments that cannot "play thy glory well," but in Meditation 2.129 he compares bagpipes to his lungs, which, if filled with Christ's "precious Aire," will allow him to pipe God's praises adequately. He also alludes to various Old Testament hymn forms, such as the michtam and hosannah, and the Hebrew musical instruments, the shoshannim and muth labben. The last couplet of most of the Meditations offers promises to praise or try to praise musically "while teather'd to my clay" (Med. 1.48).

Many of Taylor's poems also allude to or employ scientific or numerological ideas or theory, although always in service to the spiritual message. As evidenced by the collection of books in his personal library, Taylor was enthralled by such esoteric topics. His fondness for number and word games might also be connected to his experience at Harvard with Ramist logic (Haims 85), although this is still another habit of Taylor's that Grabo attempts to ally with mysticism (*Taylor* 93). Several critics suggest that the First Series stops at the forty-ninth poem just because numerological perfection would dictate an ending at the seven-times-seven multiple.[2] Taylor himself acknowledges the spiritual importance of the number seven in Meditation 2.21:

> Each Seventh Day a Sabbath Gracious Ware.
>   A Seventh Week a yearly Festivall.
> The Seventh Month a Feast nigh, all, rich fare.
>   The Seventh Yeare a Feast Sabbaticall.
>   And when seven years are seven times turnd about
>   A Jubilee. Now turn their inside out.
>
> What Secret Sweet Mysterie under the Wing
>   Of this so much Elected number lies?

The connection to the feast, allusive of the eucharist as well as to election, places this mystery securely in a Puritan rather than a mystical context.

As he does with medicinal imagery, Taylor also uses alchemical imagery often in his poems to trope the movement of man's search for salvation.[3] The power of grace to work the regeneration of the sinful soul is an obvious analogy to the alchemical distillation process, and Taylor often employs the imagery of chemical change for the fact of conversion in his poems (Clack 14). For example, in Meditation 1.34, Taylor pictures Christ as employing "gracious Chymistry" to concoct "Cordialls" out of the corpse of death, making death a remedy rather than something to be feared. Taylor also often uses the imagery of the refining process, another chemical action, that clears the dross from the precious stone of his "Inward man" (Med. 2.5).

Taylor's use of imagery, then, has a clear biblical basis, more often than not from one of the two Old Testament poetic books, the Song of Songs and the Book of Psalms. In many poems he uses the words and images from their biblical headnotes to anchor the construction of a conceit. These image clusters are those that appear most prominently in his meditative poetry.

PROSODY

Attempts to explain or characterize the prosody of Puritan poetry, to try to elicit some generalities that might create a monolithic knowledge base for understanding how Puritans wrote poetry or understood how they should write it, usually resort to speaking about "plain style." This prose structuring, used mainly in the writing of Puritan sermons, is a legacy from Petrus Ramus who influenced many New England writers. But Puritan prosody, with its reliance on biblically based technique, is far from plain. A consideration of the many linguistic devices in the Bible, particularly the kind of unsophisticated, first-hand reflections that Taylor appears to have made that allowed him to model his prosody consciously on what happens particularly in the Hebrew Old Testament poetic books, produces poetry with consistent forms that are perhaps unknown to or unappreciated by many modern readers. Taylor himself did not have access to a study of the principles of Hebrew poetics; a compendium of them was not available in the seventeenth century or before. Even Johann Buxtorf's *A Short Introduction to the Hebrew Tongue,* written in 1655 and used by the translators of the *Bay Psalm Book* as a source for their understanding of Hebrew poetic rhythm, does not specify prosodic patterns or rules. Taylor, however, appears to have examined particularly the structure of the various psalms in both Hebrew and English translation to determine their rhetorical and metrical nature, so that he could adapt some of their technique to his own verse.

A cursory reading of the meditative poetry, of course, makes it seem plain, rigid, and unvaried in its prosodic structure. Taylor's strict consistency of metrical pattern in whatever poem or series of poems he was writing seems to come from an allegiance to his own classical education rather than to what Lynn Haims sees as the spirit behind Puritan aesthetics, the anxiety and self-doubt that would pillory their sensibilities to regular metrics and rhyme (38) or what Karl Keller says is an echo of the rigidity of Taylor's Puritan faith (*Kangaroo* 53). Jeffrey Hammond sees the regularity of verse form throughout the two series of *Preparatory Meditations* as part of the ritualistic nature of the two series, while Karen Rowe sees Taylor's style as a metaphor for the soul trying to break the bonds of the body (*Sinful Self* 202, Rowe 105). Nevertheless, within this regularity is a plethora of rhetorical and figurative patterns that should divert the educated reader from the monotony of the overall stanzaic pattern.

Literary critics almost always notice Taylor's constant use of the figure of antithesis, the joining of contrasting ideas, which is most often employed in the poetry to contrast the greatness of God with the world's lowliness, which Taylor then invariably relates to his own inability to praise with suitable words. A line such as "Should Gold Wed Dung, should Stars Wooe Lobster Claws," which Taylor uses in Meditation 2.33 as an image for man's salvation, illustrates how Taylor employs antithesis throughout his poetry. This figurative technique—related to classical enantiosis, antitheton, paradox, and oxymoron[4]—is fairly common in seventeenth-century devotional poetry as a whole, and appears to derive mainly from its use by the biblical psalmist as a way of expressing humility and dependence on God. A related issue is whether Taylor, as the poetic voice of the *Preparatory Meditations,* believes himself to be at the lower end of the antithesis, in constant danger of damnation, or whether his antithetical stance reflects the conflicted but ultimately victorious path of any assured saint.

Andrew Delbanco characterizes antithetical thought as part of the New England Puritan consciousness, an ability to deal with and resolve contradiction by holding it suspended in one's head and belief system (127). Rowe sees antithesis as related to the process of typology, which not only yokes together elements in the two Testaments, but always see Christ the antitype as the superior element in the dichotomy (234–35). Barbara Lewalski sees the Meditations structured via thesis, antithesis, and resolution, with a central focus on contrasting God's greatness with Taylor's own lowliness (398); she says antithesis is a "radical technique" (402).

Taylor also often uses the related rhetorical technique of amplification, an addition to or expansion of a statement. He uses this device to counter the ultimate inexpressibility of God's being and attributes, the sticking point that so befuddles Taylor throughout the poetry and casts doubts on the legitimacy of his skill and his salvation. He uses such figures as accumulatio (the amassing of details), hyperbole (the exaggeration of qualities or numbers), and ecphonesis (emotional exclamation) to convey both the greatness of the amplified object and his own humbleness and sinfulness. Meditation 1.29 offers an example of accumulatio that expresses the wonder Taylor feels at the Incarnation:

> I being grafft in thee there up do stand
>   In us Relations all that mutuall are.
> I am thy Patient, Pupill, Servant, and
>   Thy Sister, Mother, Doove, Spouse, Son, and Heire.
>   Thou art my Priest, Physician, Prophet, King,
>   Lord, Brother, Bridegroom, Father, Ev'ry thing.

Hyperbole emerges in Meditation 1.11, as Taylor writes:

> A Deity of Love Incorporate
>   My Lord, lies in thy Flesh, in Dishes stable
> Ten thousand times more rich than golden Plate
>   In golden Services upon thy Table.

From Taylor's point of view, of course, this was not hyperbolic, as no amount of human exaggeration could approach the greatness of God, but this rhetorical technique is found often in the Book of Psalms, so Taylor— as the New England David—adapted it to his verse as a figurative attempt to reach his impossible goal. Ecphonesis, on the other hand, merely expresses Taylor's excitement or ecstasy in light of the subject of his verse or, alternately, his consternation at his own limitations: "Oh! Wealthy Theam! Oh! Feeble Phancy" (Med. 1.27). Through amplification, then, Taylor explores his theme of the contrast between the divine and the human. Humble because he is sinful and not able to praise God as He deserves, he nonetheless tries to stretch the limits of language to search for the apotheosis of praise.

Another feature of Hebrew poetry that Taylor uses throughout his verse is the iterative style, or frequent word repetition. Phrases are repeated for a quasi-incantatory effect or to express great emotion. Norman Grabo also suggests that, for the Puritan, certain words had no substitutes so only could be repeated (*Taylor* 90). The fact that the voice of God Himself uses this technique, as in Ezekiel 21 ("I will overturn, overturn, overturn it . . . A sword, a sword is drawn . . .") caught the eye of such exegetes as Martin Luther and John Calvin, who both comment positively on the use of repetition for sacred purposes. Taylor, of course, uses it too, as in Meditation 1.17:

> A King, a King, a King indeed, a King
>   Writh up in Glory! Glorie's glorious Throne
> Is glorifide by him, presented him.
>   And all the Crowns of Glory are his own.

His use of the classical rhetorical figure of ploce, often productive of a musical effect, is most likely an imitation Taylor makes of the technique David the psalmist uses in the Book of Psalms. In Meditation 1.20 he even uses the same words as those in Psalm 47: "Sing Praise, sing Praise,

sing Praise, sing Praises out, / Unto our King sing praise. . . ." He also
uses the related device polyptoton—repeating forms of the same word in
close proximity—in such poems as Meditation 2.35:

> We have our Souls undone, Can't undo this.
>   We have Undone the Law, this can't undo:
> We have undone the World, when did amiss,
>   We can't undoe the Curse that brings in Woe.
>   Our Undo-Doing can't undo, its true.
>   Wee can't our Souls, and things undone, renew.

Repetition for emotional effect or to suggest the incantatory trance of
meditation becomes a hallmark of the *Preparatory Meditations*.

Perhaps the most notable prosodic device used in the *Preparatory Meditations*, however, which is also a common technique of Hebrew poetry, is parallelism. It is a prosodic device that Taylor uses liberally in his poetry, a repetition of grammatical structure with variant words that seems similar to accumulatio, and is tied to his habit of the conceit. However, the exact prosodic structuring that Taylor uses is based directly on psalmic parallelism. Meditation 1.19 offers a good example:

> Looke till thy Looks look Wan, my Soule; here's ground.
>   The Worlds bright Eye's dash't out: Day-Light so brave
> Bemidnighted; the sparkling sun, palde round
>   With flouring Rayes lies buri'de in its grave
>   The Candle of the World blown out, down fell.
>   Life knockt a head by Death: Heaven by Hell.

Parallelism such as this holds Taylor's poetry together structurally in a major way and gives much of it a sense of slow, repetitious, almost liturgical grandeur because the addition of information in the parallel structure is less substantive and more metaphorical and emphatic. Additionally, a close consideration of what David does in the Psalms and what Taylor does in the *Meditations* reveals that Taylor adapts several different forms of recognizable Hebrew parallelism to his verse. Synonymous parallelism allows two different expressions to stand for one fundamental thought; tautological parallelism uses actual word repetition to do the same thing (thus making it similar to basic ploce, but creating the effect of a litany). Taylor's use of this type of parallelism is ubiquitous in the poetry, as for example in Meditation 1.24: "What shall an Eagle t'catch a Fly thus run? / Or Angell Dive after a Mote ith'Sun?" or in Meditation 2.26:

> Thou wilt have all that enter do thy fold
>   Pure, Cleane, and bright, Whiter than whitest Snow
> Better refin'd than most refined Gold.

Antithetic or contrasted parallelism, on the other hand, uses the structure to offer a statement of opposites in the act of corroboration. When Taylor uses this kind of parallelism, he sometimes creates a merely linguistic contrast as he puts similar sentence elements in opposite order, as in Meditation 1.31: "Begracde with Glory, gloried with Grace." But in other poems, the word order reversal also reflects a contrast in idea, as in Meditation 1.22: "Then Saints With Angells thou wilt glorify: / And burn Lewd Men, and Divells Gloriously." This opposition between the righteous and the wicked, incorporating one of Taylor's pet subjects for antithesis, is also reminiscent of this major theme in the Book of Psalms. Taylor also often uses synthetic parallelism, which intensifies or builds the idea rather than merely repeating it, using a variety of logical devices. For example, in Meditation 1.41, his parallelism is shaped for a clear cause-effect relationship: "The Magnet of all Admiration's here. / Your tumbling thoughts turn here." Taylor takes fullest advantage of synthetic parallelism in his typological meditations, however, as he creates a cause-effect relationship between the Old Testament type and Christ as the antitype. Ivy Schweitzer notes this particular use of synthetic parallelism in Taylor's verse, although she doesn't recognize it as the Hebrew technique (101). A final kind of parallelism in which the idea is slowly developed by repetition of the last half of the primary element in the first half of the secondary element, creating a ponderous effect, is called anadiplosis or steps parallelism. This type of parallelism was used for Hebrew songs meant for temple processions, such as the Songs of Ascent in the Book of Psalms. Taylor uses it also, as in Meditation 2.72:

> Hence make my Life, Lord, keep thine Honour bright.
>   And let thine Honour brighten mee by grace.
> And make thy Grace in mee, thee honour right.
>   And let not mee thy Honour ere deface.

Perhaps the most noticeable use of different forms of parallelism occurs in the occasional poem "Huswifery." The poem begins by using antithetic, then simple, then steps parallelism altogether in one verse:

> Make me, O Lord, thy Spining Wheele compleate.
>   Thy Holy Worde my Distaff make for mee.
> Make mine Affections thy Swift Flyers neate
>   And make my Soule thy holy Spoole to bee.
>   My Conversation make to be thy Reele
>   And reele the yarn thereon spun of thy Wheele.

A close look at all Taylor's work will reveal the ubiquitous use of the Hebrew device of poetic parallelism, done so intricately that he must have been conscious of imitating the technique he observed in the words of the psalter.

Another prosodic device that goes beyond the actual structuring of the verse is point of view or stance, by which a poet can betray his relationship to his intended audience as well as his attitude and mood in any given poem. Because Taylor's intended audience in the *Preparatory Meditations* and most of the occasional poems is most often wholly or partially his Lord, his first person addresses seem to have a clear sense of purpose. In the body of the meditative poetry, three stances toward his audience Christ can be identified: lament, supplication, and thanksgiving and praise, which are also the three points of view that biblical critics find in the Book of Psalms. Throughout the two series, Taylor shifts between these stances, sometimes in the body of the same poem.

The lament, a point of view intended to arouse God's pity and remind Him of His covenantal obligation, consists of several stages, some of which reflect the pattern of typical meditative poetry. The lamenting poet will cry for help, present the substance of his complaint, express his faith and trust in God, tell God what he wants, and then end with a vow to praise God if his complaints are remedied. The language of self-deprecation becomes a regular part of this point of view. A substantial number of Taylor's poems, particularly those that concentrate upon his own sins and unworthiness, are patterned as laments. Thomas Davis sees the tendency of the poems at the end of the First Series—beginning with agitation and ending with peace—to be in the style of psalmic laments (*Reading* 123). Taylor employs this stance, for example, in Meditation 1.36. He begins with a question to his audience, Christ, that could qualify as a cry for help and is fraught with the language of self-deprecation:

What rocky heart is mine? My pincky Eyes
   Thy Grace spy blancht, Lord, in immensitie.
But finde the Sight me not to meliorize,
   O Stupid Heart! What strang-strange thing am I?

He then focuses on the substance of his complaint, which in this Meditation is his typical problem of confronting the gulf between the kindness
of Christ and his own vileness, a chasm that leads Taylor to speculate
"am I not thine own?" But after this heartfelt question, Taylor goes on to
the third stage of the typical lament by expressing his faith in God:

My Faith therefore doth all these Pleas disdain.
   Thou kindness art, it saith, and I am thine.
   Upon this banck it doth on tiptoes stand
   To ken o're Reasons head at Graces hand.

After several more verses of contemplation on his theme, Taylor ends the
poem with a promise to praise:

But that there is a Crevice for one hope
   To creep in, and this Message to Convay
That I am thine, makes me refresh. Lord ope
   The Doore so wide that Love may Scip, and play.
   My Spirits then shall dance thy Praise. I'me thine.
   And Present things with things to come are mine.

Thus, although the lament is essentially a negative and self-doubting
stance, its ending is characteristically more confident as it promises to
praise.

   The structure of the supplication is only slightly different from the
lament. Indeed, biblical critics who identify this type of poem in the Book
of Psalms often classify it as a subcategory of the lament. The difference
is that the supplication poem is a petition spoken in a mood of confidence
throughout, avoiding all but the mildest self-deprecation. It begins with
a short opening invocation, followed by a description of the poet's attempts to follow God's laws or desires and what he therefore wishes God
to grant him, and a final voiced realization of the possibility of God's
help, sometimes coupled with a promise to praise. "Huswifery" stands as
a perfect example of a supplication. In the meditative poetry, those poems

in which Taylor encounters the paradox created by the duty to praise and the difficulties of doing so most obviously reflect this stance. His petition, of course, is the primary desire to find the right words to praise Christ. Meditation 1.21 is structured as a supplication. The opening invocation is in interrogative form: "What Glory's this, my Lord?" The poet follows with an account of his desires to be a better poet mixed with protestations of the sincerity of his attempts to do right:

> Oh! Bright! Bright thing! I fain would something say:
>   Lest Silence should indict me. Yet I feare
> To say a Syllable lest at thy day
>   I be presented for my Tattling here.
>   Course Phancy, Ragged Faculties, alas!
>   And Blunted Tongue don't Suit: Sighs Soile the Glass.
>
> Yet shall my mouth stand ope, and Lips let run
>   Out gliding Eloquence on each light thing?
> And shall I gag my mouth, and ty my Tongue,
>   When such bright Glory glorifies within?
>   That makes my Heart leape, dancing to thy Lute?
>   And shall my tell tale tongue become a Mute?

Taylor's mood here is essentially one of confidence despite the comparatively mild deprecation of his poetic skill, perhaps the last confident poem in the First Series as his mood after this poem quickly descends and his doubts multiply. He follows this with a more assured stanza that ends with the requisite couplet of praise:

> Lord spare I pray, though my attempts let fall
>   A slippery Verse upon thy Royall Glory.
> I'le bring unto thine Altar th'best of all
>   My Flock affords. I have no better Story.
>   I'le at thy Glory my dark Candle light:
>   Not to descry the Sun, but use by night.

He then ends this poem with an example of his attempt to accomplish his desire, two stanzas that describe the glory of God and the beauty of heaven, which leave the reader aware of Taylor's occasional confidence in his poetic ability, despite the limitations of human language.

The last classification of stance that Taylor uses is that of thanksgiving and praise. This kind of poem has a three-part structure, making it appear to imitate the structure of the typical meditation. The first part is an exclamation of intention to praise, followed by an explanation of the grounds for praise, and ending with a final statement of praise. Taylor's poems that concentrate more on God's actions than on Taylor's own sins or attempts to determine his salvation are structured as thanksgivings and praises. Meditation 1.10 is an example of this mode. The poem begins with an example of ecphonesis that qualifies as an exclamation of intention to praise: "Stupendious Love! All Saints Astonishment!" He then writes several verses that attempt to explain the extent of God's glory, and the kindness with which he has cured Taylor's spiritual "Ague." This in turn leads Taylor to an explanation of his pet theme, the Incarnation:

> But how it came, amazeth all Communion.
>   Gods onely Son doth hug Humanity,
> Into his very person. By which Union
>   His Humane Veans its golden gutters ly.
>   And rather than my Soule should dy by thirst,
>   These Golden Pipes, to give me drink, did burst.

His final statement of praise is uncharacteristically indirect: "Then make my life, Lord, to thy praise proceed / For thy rich blood, which is my Drink-Indeed."

The frequency with which Taylor uses one of these stances or a combination of two or three of them indicates that, although the poetry is clearly meditative, the structuring principle of the *Preparatory Meditations* is the Book of Psalms, as these three structures can clearly be seen to dominate that poetry as well. Moreover, Taylor uses these stances in his occasional poetry as well.

Another feature of Taylor's poetry that is based on what he observed in the Book of Psalms is a shifting of the poetic voice and the addressee within the walls of the same poem. Although Christ is most often the intended audience of Taylor's lines, this is not always so. Karl Keller tries to say his inability to stick with the same addressee shows that Taylor can't get a grip on his own identity (Keller, "Taylor" 193), but when one compares what David the psalmist does with what Taylor is doing, the shifts seem far more to be another deliberate imitation of this sanctioned book of poetry.

Of course, in *Gods Determinations* such shifts are expected, as Taylor has divided the poem into various subpoems. The preface begins with a third-person objective narration to a general audience, and the next poem continues that way as it attempts to set forth the background of the entire poem. Other poems in the piece are also narrated objectively, revealing the largely public nature of the poem and its apocalyptic subject matter of the Last Judgment. Additionally, Taylor's intentions as author are not that far away from those of a preacher. However, the third poem is a dialogue, as in a play, between Justice and Mercy, and later in the poem, there are several other dialogues, one between "Satan" and "Soul," one between "Rank Two" and "Rank Three" of those called to the Last Judgment, and four others between "Soul" and "Saint." In each case, the participants in the dialogue address each other and there is no poetic narrator. Additionally, we have two poems in which the Soul addresses Christ, two in which Christ replies to the Soul, poems directed objectively at the "Inward Man," the "Outward Man," and "The Soul," and poems in the voice of the Elect and the second and third rank of people who are still awaiting revelation of their election, all of which are directed to Christ. In the middle of the poem, two subpoems in the voice of Satan are also addressed to the second and third ranks, respectively, and in the latter part of the poem, a series of subpoems are written objectively about the Soul or directed by the voice of the Soul to Christ. On a few occasions, moreover, the addressees shift slightly within a single poem, such as with the couplet of praise directed at Christ at the end of the subpoem "Our Insufficiency to Praise God suitably, for his Mercy."

In the *Preparatory Meditations*, which could be viewed even more so than *Gods Determinations* as a seamless piece of work, the shifts of addressee become far more noticeable. They are often abrupt, creating a somewhat startling and confusing effect. Taylor sometimes interrupts his usual address of Christ or God by speaking to his own soul, as in Meditation 1.12: "But is this so? My Peuling soul then pine / In Love untill this Lovely one be thine." Yet rarely is an entire meditation addressed to his soul. In Meditation 2.68[B], for example, he begins with an address to the soul that continues through the first five stanzas:

> My megre Soule, when wilt thou fleshed bee,
>   With Spirituall plumpness? Serpents flesh dost eat
> Which maketh leane? Thy bones stick out in thee.
>   Art thou Consumptive? And Concoctst not meat?

In the fourth stanza, however, he also begins to speak of souls in general and the benefits they garner from contact with Christ. The penultimate stanza ends with this couplet:

My little Pipkin Soule of heavenly Clay
Shall fatted to the brim with grace grow gay.

These lines provide a bridge to the shift in the last stanza, which becomes
a direct address to Christ: "My Heade, O Sun, hide in thy healing Wing."
Such shifts are effective means of conveying the self-examining chastisement characteristic of the penitent Puritan in his Christian walk.

As is obvious, the shift in addressee in the context of a poem cannot
really be discussed without also mentioning shifts in the identity of the
poetic voice itself. The movement between sin and grace is not consistently a private matter in the *Meditations* delivered by a lyric persona, the
voice of the Christian poet who is Edward Taylor. The voice of the poems
does not articulate merely an individual struggle for assurance and worthy
communion with God. In several Meditations, a public voice emerges
and blends with or else temporarily replaces the private persona. Both
the public and private voices, of course, articulate the hope-doubt dilemma that is the central theme of the *Meditations,* so that in essence
Taylor's voice becomes, as Norman Grabo maintains, that of the "representative saint" who confesses his sinful carnality as the condition of all
God's Elect on earth (Taylor, *Treatise* xlv–xlvi).

In several Meditations, Taylor changes the person of his speaker by
shifting between first person singular and plural. When he does so, Taylor
creates a poem both public and personal. In Meditation 1.27, for example,
he first speaks of the redemption in communal terms:

This Flower [Christ] that in his Bosom [God's] sticks so fast,
    Stuck in the Bosom of such stuffe as wee
    That both his Purse, and all his Treasure thus,
    Should be so full, and freely sent to us.

In the next stanza, however, he considers the redemption as it applies to
himself alone: "Let him in Whom all Fulness Dwells, dwell, Lord / Within
my Heart: this Treasure therein lay." Since the universality of the experience of salvation is also ultimately an individual matter, Taylor's plural-
to-singular shift is one from public to private voice, but at the same time
reflects an experience that every Christian must go through. Such a persona who embodies the fate of all men in his own experience appears in
Meditation 1.31:

Begracde with Glory, gloried with Grace,
   In Paradise I was, when all Sweet Shines
Hung dangling on this Rosy World to face
   Mine Eyes, and Nose, and Charm mine Eares with Chimes.
   All these were golden Tills the which did hold
   My evidences wrapt in glorious folds.

But as a Chrystall Glass, I broke, and lost
   That Grace, and Glory I was fashion'd in
And cast this Rosy World with all its Cost
   Into the Dunghill Pit, and Puddle Sin.
   All right I lost in all Good things, each thing
   I had did hand a Vean of Venom in.

The fall of man, as described in the poem, is at once both personal and communal. The singular "I" stands for both Taylor individually and all men collectively. Later in the poem, the voice merges into first person plural: "What e're we want, we cannot Cry for, nay, / If that we could, we could not have it thus." The representative Christian soul and the individual here both experience redemption, as the voice assumes the plural pronoun. Thus, the collective "I" can speak in Taylor's poetry in either the singular or the plural; Taylor himself is, of course, one member of this "I" and, as such, also embodies it.

NOTES

1. For a full discussion of the intellectual development of this image cluster, see Jeske 30–33, 47–48.

2. These critics include Gatta 143; Hammond, *Fifty* 25; Gelpi 33; and Hambrick-Stowe 55.

3. Cheryl Oreowicz uses Meditation 1.7 to explain Taylor's spiritual use of alchemical imagery (108).

4. I would like to thank the editors of the Web site "Silva Rhetoricae: The Forest of Rhetoric," compiling the ongoing work of Gideon O. Burton, for these classical rhetorical terms.

7 Reception

EARLY CRITICAL RECEPTION

The earliest serious Taylor critics, most notably Perry Miller and Norman S. Grabo, were unsure about how to classify his poetry, particularly the meditative lyrics. Many of Taylor's themes and much of his meaning—his concentration on the mystery of the Incarnation, his metaphorical depiction of Christ as a bridegroom wooing Taylor as bride, his use of the emblem book tradition, and the startling vision described in the titled poems—garnered Taylor an early reputation as a mystic, whose ideas as expressed in his poetry put him closer to the Anglicans or even the Catholics (that his prose indicates were despised by him) than to the orthodox Puritans among whom he lived. Even in his revised Twayne critical book that was published in 1988, long after the debut of the painstaking criticism that traces the chief biblical and Protestant exegetical sources of Taylor's work, Grabo continues to maintain that Taylor became acquainted with Catholic meditative practices in England, where they had been introduced even to dissenters by the Jesuits. He also sees the British metaphysicals as conversant with such Catholic meditative writers as St. Ignatius Loyola, Francis de Sales, and Lorenzo Scupoli (*Taylor* 34–35, 96–97), and then posits their influence on Taylor. Grabo also sees some of Taylor's ideas as identical to those of the fourteenth-century mystic Meister Eckhart (*Taylor* 23–24).

Other early critics proclaimed Taylor as a closet Arminian, an anti-Calvinist who did not believe in the unconditionality of predestination, but who saw the act of faith in God, and not God's incontrovertible will, as a precondition of election that was worth proclaiming constantly in the hopes of influencing God's decision. This stance, of course, is very close to the Catholic belief that the covenant of works was still operative in Christian life, the main reason why their faith was suspect in the eyes of Puritans like Taylor. The earlier Meditations, especially "The Experience," were at first interpreted as similar to the Catholic Richard Crashaw's and Henry Vaughan's, as they seemed to beg Christ for a typical mystical union with Him. Jeffrey Hammond attributes this early attitude about Taylor to the limited number of poems that were available before the Donald Stanford edition was published, poems chosen by Thomas Johnson just because of their imagistic and thematic similarity to those of the British devotional poets (*Fifty* 20). Additionally, Taylor's meditative poetry about the beauty of the Supper can often seem to show allegiance to the Catholic doctrine of transubstantiation, but as Kathleen Blake indicates in her 1971 article, the Protestant alternative of consubstantiation—although very similar—suggests only a metaphorical connection between the actual bread and wine and the body and blood of Christ. This metaphorical mode of contrastive thinking is more conducive to the Ramist rationality that undergirds Protestant poetics, but it also supports the emotional rapture Taylor expresses when he writes poetry about the Supper, a rapture that is not intended to be mystical or to suggest that anyone could convert physical reality into something it is not (Blake 22). Rather, the physical substance of bread and wine is, like language, a sign of a conceptual—in this case, spiritual—reality. With Taylor's view of the Supper as an ecstatic experience of the converted soul, a completely orthodox Puritan view, it is easy for a modern reader to confuse Puritan desire with Catholic doctrine. However, in Meditation 2.108, in the anti-Stoddard series of poems, Taylor makes his position on this doctrinal issue clear to a fault:

It Consubstantiation too Confounds.
    Bread still is bread, Wine still is wine its sure.
It Transubstantiation deadly wounds.
    Your touch, Tast, Sight say true. The Pope's a whore.
    Can Bread and Wine by words be Carnifide?
    And manifestly bread and Wine abide?

Many of these early attempts to place Taylor too securely in the line of Continental and British devotional writing ignored the fact that the Catholics, or Papists, were Puritan enemies and even the Anglicans, though the Massachusetts Bay colony Puritans had not separated from that church, were considered to have less-than-perfect Christian ideas. Even as early as the writings of John Calvin, consubstantiation was perceived as the more proper way to understand the eucharist, a view of the presence of Christ spiritually rather than corporeally in the sacrament (Blake 6). Blake tells us that in this verse from Meditation 2.108, Taylor takes the position that the Puritans had adopted from the Anglican Church and the first English Prayer Book, that the bread and wine are representations of Christ and not His actual body and blood (8). As early as 1970, Ursula Brumm clarified the difference between Catholic mysticism and Puritan thought about the eucharist, explaining how the Puritans believed in an analogic view of reality, a "dialectical conception," in which such real world items as bread could also be symbols of spiritual truth, but not physically the same (Brumm, *American* 60, 74). Later work on the nature of Protestant meditation gradually got critics to realize that this religious orientation, coupled with the emotional lyricism of Taylor's natural poetic style, was at the root of such apparent mysticism that resulted in a confusion about his religious allegiance (Hammond, *Fifty* 75).

As these early critics tried to read Taylor's poems from the formalist standpoint that adulated the more imagistic aspects of the seventeenth-century British devotional framework, Taylor more often than not was labeled a minor poet and castigated for the failings of his poetry to measure up to the court-inspired smoothness of such British poets as John Donne and George Herbert. The same isolation from Britain that made him an American rara avis to some made him a failed metaphysical to others. Still others preferred to argue about whether Taylor was a metaphysical or a baroque poet, resorting to labels and literary handbook definitions but getting far away from the actual themes and sources of the poetry itself. Even as late as 1988, Grabo was trying to connect Taylor's work with that of Sor Juana Ines de la Cruz (*Taylor* 118–19). Her poetry reflects the high culture of the seventeenth-century court life of Mexico City, buoyed financially by Spanish wealth accrued from exploiting the resources of the New World. Although her religious orientation is at least partially sincere, it reflects Spanish Catholicism, which is even further in spirit and orientation from Taylor's work than British Catholicism and Anglicanism were.

MODERN CRITICAL APPROACHES

As Taylor criticism began to surface from the formalist-inspired negativity and critics began to approach Taylor's work on its own terms, or on the terms of seventeenth-century New England aesthetics, much more positive judgments of the poetry were forthcoming. Jeffrey Hammond isolates five main types of positive criticism and interpretation of Taylor's poetic canon that began in the late 1980s and early 1990s: that which attempted to define Taylor's poetry by also unearthing, exploring, and delineating the standards of Puritan aesthetics; that which considered what was known of Taylor's biography and how it had an impact on what and how he wrote; that which studied possible sources for Taylor's prosody and imagery in texts with which he would have been familiar; that which placed Taylor's work more solidly in its own cultural milieu; and that which approached the work psychologically, particularly with reference to gender theory (*Fifty* 124).

Charles Mignon and Sargent Bush Jr. were the first critics to refute the Taylor-as-mystic thesis and to see his poetry as modeled more on biblical precedent than on imitation of British devotional poets whose work we had no proof that he had ever read (Hammond, *Fifty* 57). The earliest detailed criticism of Taylor's work that related it to biblical structures and themes came from the German critics Ursula Brumm and Peter Nicolaisen. Hammond notes that close attention to biblical hermeneutics and the Bible as literature came initially from German scholars, which may have made Brumm and Nicolaisen more sensitive to these origins of Taylor's thought (*Fifty* 50–51). Karen Rowe added to this thread of criticism by deliberately differentiating Taylor's techniques from that of the metaphysicals by establishing that the basis of his image structures and what appear to be the complex conceits of his ideas have their source in typology, drawn strictly from a biblical view of religious history where Christ, as antitype, is always superior (138–39).

It was Hammond himself who began the movement of Taylor criticism not only toward the Bible but also toward the commentary and exegetical traditions that Taylor would have been familiar with. His doctoral dissertation, "Songs from the Garden: Edward Taylor and the Canticles," and the several published articles that emerged from it in the next few years carefully investigate and interpret the exegesis on the Song of Songs with which Taylor was familiar and demonstrate how the poet turns this exegetical knowledge into poetic images and themes. Rosemary Fithian Guruswamy's work on the Psalms also explores the many psalm paraphrases (with introductions) and commentaries on the Psalms with which Taylor would have been familiar, as well as his own work on the Psalms in the form of psalm paraphrases and his experience with psalmody in his everyday life, and then demonstrates that the *Preparatory Meditations* and the valedictory poems were both modeled with Taylor's full consciousness of where the exegesis placed biblical poetry in conjunction with good Puritans' poetic impulses, as well as what Taylor would have been able to deduce about Hebrew prosodic and imagistic structure from a careful reading of the psalter. Although other work investigated particular biblical passages and how a Puritan would have interpreted them as well as how common biblically based practices such as Christology would have influenced Taylor's perception of the Bible and how he used it in the construction of his poetry, Rowe's, Hammond's, and Guruswamy's work demonstrate conclusively that the poetic books of the Bible were Taylor's major inspiration.

The most recent and comprehensive book about Edward Taylor's poetry that reflects most, if not all, of the five types of criticism outlined by Hammond, is a 1997 collection prepared by a group of Taylor scholars entitled *The Tayloring Shop*, edited by Michael Schuldiner. This work is actually a festschrift to honor the retirement of Thomas M. Davis, prepared by a group of current academics who were his former students and who, in the mid-1970s, worked with him on various theses and dissertations that drew from the primary Taylor scholarship with which Davis himself was involved. The book also honors the complementary work of Virginia L. Davis, who assisted her husband in the discovery and transcription of the body of Taylor's minor poetry and important prose works and did the preliminary investigation of his relationship to music and the *Bay Psalm Book*. In *The Tayloring Shop*'s introduction, Schuldiner announces the focus of the six articles, which is to explore the several literary and cultural traditions with which Taylor would have been familiar in his lifetime and that informed the writing of his poetry. Schuldiner also emphasizes the modernity of the essays, as they update many of the critical assumptions made by earlier Taylor scholars that have since proven to be untrue or only partially true. By using this approach, the book is able to present Taylor's poetry positively within the context of its own times and without any baggage from twentieth- or twenty-first-century critical expectations.

The first two articles explore traditions associated with the *Preparatory Meditations*. Jeffrey Jeske writes about Taylor's knowledge of the contemporary zeitgeist surrounding the "book of nature" and demonstrates that the development of Taylor's attitude toward nature in his poetry actually reverses the historical modernization of these ideas, offering increased evidence for Taylor's conservatism. Thus, Taylor is shown to have a highly religious view of nature, subject to his opinions about man's carnality, which explains the lack of attention he pays in his poetry to the wilderness around him and its impact on his life. Raymond Craig then explores New England Puritan exegesis on biblical intertextuality and how that exegesis had an impact on Taylor's poetry. His extensive familiarity with scripture and his constant work with exegetical texts and commentaries are thus seen as positive influences on his poetry.

Articles by Schuldiner and J. Daniel Patterson focus on *Gods Determinations*. Schuldiner traces Taylor's use of the Puritan philosophical technique of casuistry and its relationship to the structure of the three covenants in the poem, showing how Taylor often employs the structures of sermon technique in the construction of his poems. Patterson then demonstrates how sermon structure and rhetoric inform the ponderous style of *Gods Determinations*, making it seem more like a public poem, as various critics have surmised, and obviating the necessity to compare it unfavorably to the meditative poems.

The final two articles consider Taylor's minor poetry. Jeffrey Hammond demonstrates how Taylor's elegies are examples of the New England elegiac tradition, which differs from the British Renaissance tradition of the pastoral elegy. As public poems, their structure and imagery were acceptable to the genre and to Taylor's contemporary audience. Rosemary Fithian Guruswamy, in the final article, shows how Taylor's valedictory poems are modeled on Psalm 19. Her article illustrates not only the poems' indebtedness to the biblical book but also how Taylor's imagination and New Israelite consciousness remained active even in the later stages of his life.

All articles begin with lengthy considerations of the tradition, which they then ally to Taylor's poetry, attempting to create an overall picture of the cultural and theological milieu in which Taylor wrote and in which they themselves were immersed during their graduate studies and into their professional careers.

The attention paid to the influence of the Bible, which led critics to realize how biblically based a society Taylor lived in, led the most contemporary Taylor critics to explore Taylor, often from a current theoretical hermeneutic such as reader response or cultural criticism, within the context of his own culture. Jeffrey Hammond leads his readers away from a twentieth-century appraisal of Taylor's poetry to see how Taylor's own potential Puritan audience or else his own concept of Christ as the intended reader of his meditative poetry would consider the aesthetics and emotional meaning of Taylor's works. Hammond has written both about the more personal meditative poetry as well as the elegies, which he sees as performing a public cultural function for Taylor and the Puritans whose relatives he is eulogizing. Karen Rowe also places Taylor within the context of the traditions of his own times, but unlike Hammond, who finds Taylor to be a good enough poet for his own culture, Rowe still wishes to see him as a visionary singer. Others such as Michael Clark attempt to focus on Taylor's language use within the context of poststructuralist ideas about the nature of language and thought.

8 Bibliographical Essay

Four of the earliest books that considered the works of Edward Taylor set the groundwork for all further study. Norman S. Grabo's Twayne volume *Edward Taylor* was published in 1961, just one year after Donald E. Stanford's edition of Taylor's poetry appeared. After some time, William J. Scheick and Karl Keller published within a two-year span (1974 and 1975, respectively) the first two critical works that tried to make sense of the idea structure behind the writing of Taylor's poetry. Finally, Barbara K. Lewalski furthered our knowledge about Taylor's poetic production and set him properly within the context of his British contemporaries in her 1979 volume *Protestant Poetics and the Seventeenth Century Religious Lyric*.

NORMAN S. GRABO

Although his preface chronicles the critical and cultural changes that have affected literary criticism since he published the first edition of *Edward Taylor* in the Twayne United States Authors Series in 1961—the first book-length study of Taylor—Norman S. Grabo then admits that the 1988 revised edition departs little from how he analyzes the works of Edward Taylor. Two of his main contentions remain unaltered in any major way: in this book, Grabo still uses the traditions of medieval Catholic mysticism to explain much of what he sees Taylor doing in the poetry (although he no longer claims that Taylor himself was a closet Catholic, but only a Puritan who wishes that the same mystical traditions applied to his own religion), and he also remains convinced that somewhere out there a sermon exists as a companion for every meditative poem that Taylor wrote. The volume begins with a helpful chronology of known biographical facts about Taylor. The chapters that detail his life more extensively, in the tradition of the Twayne series, are divided between his life in the world as an educated Puritan, a frontier minister, and an orthodox defender of the old New England way, and his contemplative life as a Puritan devotional thinker and writer. Grabo makes the case for his uniqueness as a bright and exciting poet in an otherwise gloomy time and place. Grabo's intelligent analysis of Taylor's poetic voice draws together the different and often contradictory strains of Puritanism in the wilderness. He depicts a poet who follows his community's predetermined path of justification, sanctification, and anticipation of glorification, who knows and responds to the meditative tradition and the faculty psychology inherited from England, as well as to the classical and Ramist logic taught to him at Harvard and perhaps earlier at Cambridge. Much of what Grabo depicts as the "mystic way" relates more to Protestant meditative techniques than Grabo appears to want to admit, although his knowledge of meditative theory and technique in the seventeenth century is vast.

In his third chapter, Grabo illuminates the connections he sees between Taylor's sermons and his poems. This chapter also contains a consideration of Taylor's attitude toward language, rhetoric, symbolism, and metaphor in the face of using them to praise such a mighty God. Grabo concludes rightly that Taylor's perception of the hypostatic union is what motivates him to be able to compose poetry, seeing the correspondence between the human and the godly that allows Taylor to perform what he sees as his poetic duty. In chapter 4, "Accomplishment," Grabo analyzes the different types of poetry that Taylor wrote, starting with some "non-devotional" poems, which include his elegies and more personal poems, continuing with the *Preparatory Meditations* (including speculation about several sources that might have inspired Taylor to begin writing them as well as an in-depth consideration of the emblem book tradition and its effect on Taylor's imagery), and ending with an analysis of *Gods Determinations*, which he defines as a "rhapsody" or a "purposely ragged stitching together of sometimes quite disparate materials" (100).

Grabo's last chapter comprises an appraisal of Taylor's work and the effect it has had on the way scholars think of American colonial literature. He suggests that Taylor's poetry has started a discussion about the structure of Puritan aesthetics. Subsequently, he traces the history of Taylor scholarship since the publication of the first edition of *Edward Taylor*, including some other prominent critics of Taylor's work.

WILLIAM J. SCHEICK

William J. Scheick's volume *The Will and the Word: The Poetry of Edward Taylor* attempts to explain the modus operandi behind what Taylor does mainly in the *Preparatory Meditations* by looking at the philosophy of early Christian writers, most noticeably Saint Augustine and his theory of the faculties of the soul. In the book, Scheick establishes the highly personal nature of the self-examination Taylor appears to undergo as he writes his meditative series and he views Taylor's search for salvation as a "quest for love." Scheick sees the faculty of the will as central to Taylor's expressions of doubt, assurance, and love, and states that Taylor credits man with volitional power to turn desires from carnality to the spiritual, even though predestination mandates that he can do nothing to effect his own salvation. Scheick also explores the value of the faculty of reason in early Christian and Puritan philosophy and its juxtaposition to a stance of faith. He includes a discussion of Puritan views of the human body, which he sees as leading Taylor to an acknowledgment of the importance of the Incarnation because it took away the stigma of sinfulness from the human body.

In the second part of the book, Scheick turns to a discussion of Taylor's view of the Word made flesh and its connection to the words he was attempting to put on paper to describe his Lord. He makes the assumption that Taylor modeled his poetry after contemporary meditative practices, and cites Richard Baxter's *Saints Everlasting Rest* as a chief influence on Taylor's writing. Scheick suggests that Taylor combined his Christologically centered exegetical knowledge of the Bible with linguistic beliefs that focused on the efficacy of Jesus as the Word made Flesh, explaining this again with the use of early Christian theology. Metaphor, then, as a yoking together of unlike things, was to Taylor a linguistic parallel to the work that God had done in arranging Christ's redemptive act, and this is what legitimated Taylor using his gift to praise the Lord.

Scheick deftly lays the groundwork in this book by which later critics would delineate Taylor's central themes and his connection to early Christian exegesis. He allows us to see that Taylor was a student of the Bible, and that his Puritanism did not ban from his repertoire a consideration of nature and the body.

KARL KELLER

Karl Keller's book *The Example of Edward Taylor* attempts in a very imaginative way to depict Taylor as the first poet in an American tradition and an example for future poets, even though they could not possibly have read his work. Keller posits that Taylor's immersion in the premiere stages of American culture, the Puritan experience in the American wilderness, made him essentially the first significant poet in America. He endeavors to get the reader to know Taylor by dividing the biographical information that was accessible in the early 1970s into the categories of a student, a dissenter from the mainstream Protestant religion and defender of the Puritan strain, the minister of the Westfield congregation, a husband and father who wrote limited poetry about that domestic experience, a pioneer on the New England frontier, an amateur doctor and scientist, and finally a poet. He then attempts to detail and prove his thesis, that Taylor belongs solidly at the beginning of the American tradition of poetry due to his allegiance to orthodox New England theology and its intended creation of an American theocracy, the first stage of the many guises of American nationalism. He ends the introductory chapters by making a rather loose attempt to tie together the concern of the *Preparatory Meditations* with the process of writing poetry, the process orientation endemic to the search for one's spiritual fate in the theology of Puritanism, and Taylor's American traditionalism by explaining how process also operates in such phenomena as the American skyscraper and the unresolved harmonies of American jazz.

In chapter 4, Keller categorizes the poetry and discusses several themes he sees in Taylor's verse that are now commonplaces in Taylor scholarship: its private meditative and spiritually intense nature, Taylor's view of his own words as related to his spiritual fate, and the movement from sin to song. Later, Keller also explores the poetry's connection to the Lord's Supper. His most central hypothesis, however, is that the poetry is mythical, and that the poetic persona Taylor creates is an act or a drama of salvation that is meant to be representative more than personal and is the embodiment of the Connecticut Valley Puritan, a topic he explores more extensively, as well as more abstractly, in chapter 9. He also considers Taylor's prose in the same chapter, which he finds far less interesting because of its single-minded preoccupation with doctrinal issues and nothing meditative or personal.

In chapters 5 through 8 Keller looks at specific poems separately, *Gods Determinations*, the "Metrical History of Christianity," and the *Preparatory Meditations*, respectively, the latter of which comprises two chapters. In response to Stanford's edition, Keller finds *Gods Determinations* to be a lesser work of Taylor's in light of the meditative poetry. He stresses the doctrinal nature of the poem and its concern with Taylor's church life and the particular situation of the New England congregations. He views the poem, as many critics after him do, as a public document meant for Taylor's fellow church members to read. He also notes that Taylor in the poem is both preacher and church member, employing a variety of voices although not using the emotional excesses of the meditative verse. Chapter 5 concludes with Keller's attempt to ally this poem with the darker side of American literature, depicted more popularly in Nathaniel Hawthorne's short stories or Emily Dickinson's verse. In chapter 6, Keller finds the "Metrical History" to be a unique poem that could have been written, he declares, by nobody else in colonial New England but Taylor. He proceeds with a careful and detailed description and analysis of the poem, but concludes that it is essentially an embarrassment in its "annoying" antihumanism and unrelenting doggerel.

When he gets to the *Preparatory Meditations*, however, Keller's imaginative and canny view of the poetry blossoms. He labels Taylor's style in these poems as a "wilderness baroque," because of their concentration on the creation of metaphor and the use of wit. He does, however, point out that Taylor's use of domestic imagery, formulaic humility, and the occasional scatological metaphor reveals that this is American and not British baroque poetry. Keller also is the first critic to see that the process of metaphor was important to Taylor because of its parallelism to the process of the Incarnation, bringing together the Word with Taylor's beloved words. Unlike Grabo and other earlier critics, Keller does not see any mysticism in Taylor's use of meditative traditions and very few metaphysical habits in his versifying, but he faults the poet for those absences. In chapter 8, he explores Taylor's imagery, with particular attention to the scatological and erotic metaphors that gave Keller some provocative topics for earlier journal articles. He attempts to show a scriptural and exegetical history for this type of imagery, situating it as decidedly Puritan rather than the private pornography of a frustrated minister.

In the latter chapters of the book, Keller analyzes the topic of Taylor's apparent primitivism that, in his opinion, makes Taylor an essentially American poet. He cites the coarseness and irregularity of Taylor's prosody, his mixture of levels of diction, and his occasional violation of poetic convention. Then he tries to place Taylor in the tradition of classical humanism, noting that he was most certainly a Christian humanist, but that he also believed that man was potentially capable of perfection and that made him also a classical Idealist. Another thing Taylor does that, to Keller, makes him a classical humanist is that he uses language and form to create the ideal Taylor, reinforcing Keller's earlier topic of Taylor's self-mythologizing. This leads Keller to an analysis of the Incarnation and the role it plays in Taylor's poetic creations, as well as some explanation of Taylor's preparationism. Finally, Keller leads the reader back to his thesis, that Taylor took from the old to lead to the new creation of a distinctly American voice.

BARBARA K. LEWALSKI

Barbara K. Lewalski's coverage of the impulses behind the production of the seventeenth-century religious lyric is of value to both British and American seventeenth-century studies. Its primary emphasis is to establish a framework and history for Protestant poetics that would differentiate it from the Catholic mystical tradition, mainly by the increased Protestant adherence to the words of scripture. Much of the work to follow that allows critics to explore exactly what Taylor saw in scripture that allowed him to model his poetry and even permit himself to write it in the face of its human limitations and the taint of his own sin owes its motivation to Lewalski's work.

Her chapter on Taylor, "Edward Taylor: Lisps of Praise and Strategies for Self-Dispraise," identifies him as "a Protestant poet practicing a Protestant poetics" (389) and begins by discounting the commonplace assumption that he owes a literary debt to George Herbert (which, in many cases, added to the negative reception of Taylor's poetry). She points out many of the essential elements of Taylor's imagery and prosody on which later critics have elaborated: the emblemlike nature of many of his occasional poems, his closeness to the Bible in his use of imagery and metaphor (more so than any of his British contemporaries), his conservative, Christologically based use of typology, and his ubiquitous use of antithesis. She does, however, say that Taylor's *Preparatory Meditations* are basically deliberate meditative texts written in relation to sermons he was also writing and have little to do with specific biblical texts, such as the Book of Psalms or the Canticles, a supposition that has since been proven to be false and even seems to be belied by some of her own research that she discusses later in the chapter. She concludes by asserting that Taylor was the last of his kind, a Puritan writer dependent on a Protestant poetics that he helped to create.

The publication of these four important books that advanced critical knowledge and reception of Edward Taylor's poetry was accompanied by many articles published in various literary journals from the mid-1960s through the end of the 1980s. These, many of which concentrated in an explicator-type fashion on an individual Meditation or even an individual image in a Meditation, still allowed interest in Taylor to continue. In the late 1980s through the 1990s, then, six other important books turned Taylor studies in the direction of increased knowledge about the traditions that produced a poet like Edward Taylor.

KAREN ROWE

Karen Rowe's book *Saint and Singer: Edward Taylor's Typology and the Poetics of Meditation* (1986) adds detail to earlier work done on Puritan uses of typology, especially those essays collected in the 1972 Sacvan Bercovitch edition, *Typology and Early American Literature*, which features articles on Taylor's poetry by Robert E. Reiter, Karl Keller, and Ursula Brumm, as well as a general article on Puritan typology by Thomas M. Davis. Early in her volume, Rowe establishes that Taylor not only uses the exegetically sanctioned relationship of Old Testament happenings to Christ's words and actions in the New Testament but that he also "applies the perceived moral truths or correspondences to himself, a seventeenth-century Puritan operating under the gospel" (1). She then proceeds to set forth with great detail and careful research the history of Protestant typology, including the features that set it apart from the Catholic mystical tradition. She also makes the case for typology's popularity in colonial New England, most particularly during Taylor's lifetime. Most of the text is occupied with the sermons in the (at the time) newly discovered Taylor sermon collection, *Upon the Types of the Old Testament*, and close readings of the poetry that Taylor wrote on the same typological themes that characterize the sermons, most specifically the first thirty poems of the Second Series. She finds Taylor's ability to translate these sermon topics into imaginative poetry to be proof that he was "strikingly original" (37), and she also sees him turning typology into "a potent weapon" to help him deal with the heresies he detected in the New England theocracy that were the bane of his existence because they cut into the necessity of purity in the formation of the Puritan theocracy (91). Most of all, though, Rowe sees the composition of the *Preparatory Meditations*—typologically based and otherwise—as proof that Taylor was a visionary singer writing new psalms in the wilderness.

Rowe also observes that Taylor's primary impetus for writing meditative poetry was to secure his ability to administer the Lord's Supper purely and correctly to his Puritan congregation, seeing the capacity to explicate and apply typology as a major ingredient in such preparation. She points out that both Taylor and Solomon Stoddard, in their prose writing, often cite the Old Testament ceremonies and types, explicated typologically, to provide biblical proof for their stands on the issue, and she devotes a section of her chapter on "Sacramental Types" to a detailed account of the textual debate material about the communion controversy in the Thomas Prince collection. An appendix at the back of the book also includes a timeline of significant dates and events in the Taylor–Stoddard debate. She notes, as do other critics, the relatively more doctrinal nature of Meditations 2.1–30 compared with earlier Meditations, and she attributes this to Taylor's need to dispute Stoddard's position and the mental familiarity he had at the time with the prose documents he had already written or was in the process of writing about the controversy.

Toward the end of the book, Rowe turns to a discussion of Taylor's eschatological concerns and the role that typologically based poetry played in his progress toward his own glorification. She brings up what is now commonplace, that Taylor finally decided that his language would never be perfect until he was praising God among the saints in heaven, but that he appears to believe that using a biblically sanctioned technique, such as typology, represents the best he felt he could do while on earth. Rowe also establishes that Taylor thought of poetry largely in terms of music, specifically the music associated with the Book of Psalms. This continues to relate to the theme of Rowe's book, as the psalms themselves are foreshadowings in a typological sense of the songs Taylor would be able to sing in heaven. Rowe concludes her book with a substantial discussion of the Canticles Meditations, seeing Solomon as one more Old Testament type whom Taylor felt he could imitate.

JOHN GATTA

In 1989, John Gatta published *Gracious Laughter: The Meditative Wit of Edward Taylor*. The book begins with a careful delineation of what wit meant to writers in the seventeenth century, and how these writers would interpret the parodic, the comic and the high comic, based largely on early modern commonplaces and metaphysical concerns, before the advent of the neoclassical age in the eighteenth century. Still, as Gatta observes, Taylor's poetry also contains some classical comic motifs that he would have been introduced to during his study at Harvard. Gatta also discusses modern play theory and the idea of eroticism's role in wordplay, with some poststructuralist emphasis, to round out his discussion of the many features of rhetorical wit that seem to enter the style and structure of Taylor's poetry.

What the poems then become, in Gatta's opinion, are exercises in surprise, using a strange image here and an unusual turn of phrase there, to provide a "shock of joyous recognition" (56) that leaves the reader believing that Taylor's self-deprecating sinner could be nothing more than a pose to set forth with even more joy the triumph of Taylor-saint. Gatta demonstrates that Taylor deliberately uses rhetorical features common to other witty texts to show the Puritan surprise at the advent of saving grace.

Gatta also speculates that, because of his deliberate rhetorical fashioning, Taylor is writing for a definite audience, especially in *Gods Determinations*, where Gatta sees a combination of rhetorical pattern, a reversal of the jeremiad pattern so familiar to the Puritans in the many sermons they listened to and read, and the use of the comic to relieve the spiritual melancholy that plagued many Puritans, as attesting to the poem's public nature. But he conjectures further that some of the *Preparatory Meditations* might also be intended for a public audience, as edification literature to show them such things as the ecstatic truth of ascertaining one's conversion, which he sees as the theme of "The Reflexion." Furthermore, the comic nature he identifies within *Gods Determinations* he also sees as typifying the meditative poems specifically related to the Lord's Supper. He clearly makes the case that the eucharist is a festival to Taylor, and foreshadows for him the banquet feast for the Elect that awaits them in heaven.

Gatta also provides some summaries of Taylor's sources and stylistic features that are of use in developing knowledge in a more general sense of exactly where the poetry is coming from and what it is doing. These include the definition of the conceit and the role it plays in Taylor's prosodic canon, the difference between Catholic and Protestant meditative traditions, the way typology works in the poetry, the use Taylor makes of the Psalms, the Canticles, and other biblical books, the way Taylor idolizes what God has done by incarnating his Son, the problem of voice in the poetry, and how a commitment to a belief in man's essential depravity could be juxtaposed by comic verse.

THOMAS M. DAVIS

Arguably the most important book to be published about the life and work of Edward Taylor is *A Reading of Edward Taylor* by Thomas M. Davis (1992). Davis spent his academic career working on Taylor manuscripts and unearthing the traditions, both historical and biblical, that informed

Taylor's work. This study of Taylor's poetry is the culmination of Davis's decades-long investigation, prepared as he neared retirement from Kent State University.

Besides interpreting and commenting on the aesthetics of Taylor's poetry, Davis also offers a more detailed biographical and historical backdrop than had been previously available. He provides some original and interesting insights, such as his belief that the poems do not deal directly with administration of the Lord's Supper until perhaps the end of the First Series and that, at any rate, the poems may not have been composed in the consistent order that Taylor's manuscript suggests, but that the manuscript may have been reordered one or several times to reflect Taylor's intentions for the overall thematics of the collection. In many ways, Davis demonstrates, Taylor was a conscious poet concerned with the actual task of writing and rhyming, as much as with the spiritual themes and movements that the meditative poetry encompasses.

Davis also explains what he sees as the significant difference between the best poetry, which Taylor has placed early in the First Series, and the more strained and less competent poetry of the Second Series. He speculates on the reasons why Taylor turns more and more to doctrinal and religious themes and images that thin out the lyric intensity of the *Meditations*, one of which is a more rigid concern with ritual in the production of his verse. Still, Davis mounts the defense toward the end of his book that Taylor must be considered in the context of who he was, and not be judged by standards outside of his need to know and love Christ in the most sanctioned way he could through his own poetry. Davis also claims that all of Taylor's aesthetics, his imagery, his prosody, and his life itself came from the pages of scripture. Nevertheless, Davis makes a final claim for Taylor's uniqueness in the annals of American poetry as well as seventeenth-century devotional verse.

JEFFREY HAMMOND

Published in 1993, Jeffrey Hammond's *Sinful Self, Saintly Self: The Puritan Experience of Poetry* is the first full-length text to interpret the poetry of Edward Taylor through the lens of a modern theoretical approach, specifically reader response criticism and Stanley Fish's concept of the interpretive community, which Hammond defines as theological and cultural. Long invested in a belief that the negativity surrounding Taylor's reputation was a product of his being read by modernist standards, Hammond is able to employ reception theory to illustrate how Puritan poetic texts would have been perceived and read by the people who wrote them and those who were the intended readers. Using Anne Bradstreet's "As Weary Pilgrim" as a proof-text, Hammond discusses what he sees to be "modernist bias" (7), which prevents critics from realizing that jeremiads, meditations, confessional and autobiographical spiritual poetry, and verse that draws heavily on the Bible and biblical exegesis for its structure and imagery were not only acceptable, but were the stuff of poetry for the New England Puritan intent on practicing art the way Christ had revealed that He wanted it to be practiced. The intent of all Puritan writing, as Hammond says, was to cast the self in a role that would reveal imminent salvation based on biblical model and precedent. If the biblical speaker or subject was a representative saint, then the budding poet could do no better than to imitate him or her, and thus the Bible becomes a "meta-text" for the Puritan poet (19). As Hammond puts it: "The power of verse to stimulate the self's redemptive possibilities defined the Puritan experience of poetry" (34).

The following parts of the book use the poetry of Michael Wigglesworth, Bradstreet, and finally—in part 4—Edward Taylor to illustrate this thesis. Chapter 7 covers the writing of *Gods Determinations*. Hammond sees this poem as being addressed specifically to the converted who know, but perhaps in the faith-doubt continuum have forgotten, that Christ is essentially loving and merciful, and that heaven is obtained on His behalf alone. In chapter 8, "'Both Wayes Born': Edward Taylor as Weary Pilgrim," Hammond considers the occasional poems. Using "The Ebb & Flow" to characterize the emotional movement of Taylor's voice, Hammond illustrates how this cycle of cool affections and ardent pursuit of Christ characterizes the Puritan experience in all of the minor poetry. Foreshadowing his later work on the Puritan elegy, Hammond examines how Taylor performs the "elegiac duty" (180) felt to be requisite of anyone in the saved community who would write an elegy for someone sure to have been glorified who could thus serve as an example for the rest of the community awaiting their glorification.

Chapters 9 and 10 allow Hammond to look at both series of the *Preparatory Meditations*. He states that they are not without an audience, as other critics have speculated, even though they may have been intentionally kept private and unpublished. Hammond sees that Taylor writes intentionally for a reader who is the Christ that emerges from Taylor's reading of the New Testament. With this reader in mind, then, Taylor attempts to write himself into being as "the saintly metaself shaped by the interior ebb and flow of sin and grace" (189). Thus, he is not as much on the continuum himself, battered by its highs and lows, as he is presenting through language that self that the Bible told him was the type of person that God typically chose for election. The sinful part of the self, Hammond observes, similar to the voice Taylor gives to Satan in *Gods Determinations*, is a ritualistic illustration of the negligible half of the necessary equation that leads the human being to glorification. Hammond also suggests that in the imitation of the double nature of the Puritan saint, Taylor also reflects the more glorious double nature of Christ evidenced in Taylor's prized Incarnation. Additionally, this imitation allows Taylor to reach for the ultimate "intimacy with Christ that is his goal" (203).

At the beginning of chapter 10, Hammond makes the case for Taylor's use of biblical prosody and imagery as a way of projecting the metaself he has created into the Bible where he feels it belongs. He is thus able to identify with the poets of scripture, such as David and Solomon, but reaches the full apotheosis of biblical identification when, in the later Canticles sequence, he becomes the bride of Christ. The chapter ends with an interpretation of Taylor's valedictory poems in light of Hammond's overall thesis. He sees the versions of Taylor's final poem as an actual rehearsal for the glorification that he is soon to undergo.

Hammond's study does a great deal to advance a mature understanding of the Puritan aesthetic, but more than that, it foregrounds the whole body of Taylor's poetry—not to mention that of Wigglesworth and Bradstreet—as worthy of reading in the pursuit of cultural understanding.

Edward Taylor's Gods Determinations *and* Preparatory Meditations: A Critical Edition, edited by Daniel Patterson and published by Kent State University Press in winter 2002, promises to be the next major addition to the body of Taylor scholarship.

Works Cited

Blake, Kathleen. "Edward Taylor's Protestant Poetic: Nontransubstantiating Metaphor." *American Literature* 43 (March 1971): 1–24.

Brumm, Ursula. *American Thought and Religious Typology.* Trans. John Hoagland. New Brunswick: Rutgers UP, 1970.

———. "Meditative Poetry in New England." White 318–36.

Burton, Gideon O. "Silva Rhetoricae: The Forest of Rhetoric." 16 May 2002. http://www.rhetoric.byu.edu.

Caldwell, Patricia. *The Puritan Conversion Narrative: The Beginnings of American Expression.* Cambridge: Cambridge UP, 1983.

Clack, Randall A. *The Marriage of Heaven and Earth: Alchemical Regeneration in the Works of Taylor, Poe, Hawthorne, and Fuller.* Westport, CT: Greenwood P, 2000.

Clark, Michael. "The Honeyed Knot of Puritan Aesthetics." White 67–83.

Cotton, John. *God's Promise to His Plantation.* 1634. Rpt. Boston, 1686.

———. *Singing of Psalmes a Gospel Ordinance. Or a Treatise, Wherein Are Handled These Four Particulars. 1. Touching the Duty it Selfe. 2. Touching the Matter to be Sung. 3. Touching the Singers. 4. Touching the Manner of Singing.* London, 1647.

Daly, Robert. *God's Altar: The World and the Flesh in Puritan Poetry.* Berkeley: U of California P, 1978.

Davis, Thomas M. *A Reading of Edward Taylor.* Newark: U of Delaware P, 1992.

Davis, Thomas M., and Virginia L. Davis, eds. *Edward Taylor's "Church Records" and Related Sermons.* Vol. 1 of *The Unpublished Writings of Edward Taylor.* Boston: Twayne, 1981.

———. *Edward Taylor's Harmony of the Gospels.* 4 vols. Delmar, NY: Scholars' Facsimiles and Reprints, 1983.

———. *Edward Taylor's Minor Poetry*. Vol. 3 of *The Unpublished Writings of Edward Taylor*. Boston: Twayne, 1981.

Delbanco, Andrew. *The Puritan Ordeal*. Cambridge: Harvard UP, 1989.

Eberwein, Jane Donahue. "Edward Taylor." *Early American Poetry*. Ed. Jane Donahue Eberwein. Madison: U of Wisconsin P, 1978. 62–72.

Gatta, John. *Gracious Laughter: The Meditative Wit of Edward Taylor*. Columbia: U of Missouri P, 1989.

Gelpi, Albert. *The Tenth Muse: The Psyche of the American Poet*. Cambridge: Harvard UP, 1975.

Grabo, Norman S. "Editing Taylor's *Christographia* and *Treatise concerning the Lord's Supper*." *Studies in Puritan American Spirituality* 1 (1990): 13–18.

———. *Edward Taylor: Revised Edition*. Boston: Twayne, 1988.

Haims, Lynn M. "Puritan Iconography: The Art of Edward Taylor's *Gods Determinations*." White 84–98.

Hambrick-Stowe, Charles E. *Early New England Meditative Poetry: Anne Bradstreet and Edward Taylor*. New York: Paulist P, 1988.

Hammond, Jeffrey A. "'Diffusing All by Pattern': Edward Taylor as Elegist." Schuldiner 153–92.

———. *Edward Taylor: Fifty Years of Scholarship and Criticism*. Columbia, SC: Camden House, 1993.

———. *Sinful Self, Saintly Self: The Puritan Experience of Poetry*. Athens: U of Georgia P, 1993.

Hart, James D., ed. *The Oxford Companion to American Literature*. 6th ed. Rev. and add. Phillip W. Leininger. New York: Oxford UP, 1995.

Jeske, Jeff. "Edward Taylor and the Traditions of Puritan Nature Philosophy." Schuldiner 27–67.

Johnson, Thomas H. "A Seventeenth-Century Printing of Some Verses of Edward Taylor." *New England Quarterly* 14 (1941): 139–41.

Keller, Karl. "Edward Taylor, the Acting Poet." White 185–97.

———. *The Example of Edward Taylor*. Amherst: U of Massachusetts P, 1975.

———. *The Only Kangaroo among the Beauty*. Baltimore: Johns Hopkins UP, 1979.

Koelling, Deborah Spangler. "Taylor on Taylor: A Family Memoir of Edward Taylor." *Resources for American Literary Study* 12 (Spring 1982): 29–42.

Lewalski, Barbara Kiefer. *Protestant Poetics and the Seventeenth Century Religious Lyric*. Princeton: Princeton UP, 1979.

Lowance, Mason. *The Language of Canaan*. Cambridge: Harvard UP, 1980.

Martz, Louis Lohr. *The Poetry of Meditation: A Study of English Religious Literature of the Seventeenth Century*. New Haven: Yale UP, 1959.

Mather, Cotton. *A Companion for Communicants: Discourses upon . . . the Lords Supper*. Boston, 1690.

———. *Psalterium Americanum. The Book of Psalms, in a Translation Exactly Conformed unto the Original; but All in Blank Verse, Fitted unto the Tunes Commonly Used in Our Churches. . . .* Boston, 1718.

Miller, Perry, and Thomas H. Johnson, eds. *The Puritans: A Sourcebook of Their Writings*. Vol. 1. New York: Harper and Row, 1938.

Morgan, Edmund S. *Visible Saints: The History of a Puritan Idea*. New York: New York UP, 1963.

Murphy, Francis, ed. *The Diary of Edward Taylor*. Springfield, MA: Connecticut Valley Historical Museum, 1964.

———. "A Letter on Edward Taylor's Bible." *Early American Literature* 6 (1971): 91.

Oreowicz, Cheryl Z. "Investigating 'the *America* of nature': Alchemy in Early American Poetry." White 99–110.

Parker, David L. "Petrus Ramus and the Puritans: The 'Logic' of Preparationist Conversion Doctrine." *Early American Literature* 8 (1973): 140–62.

Patterson, J. Daniel. "The Homiletic Design of Edward Taylor's *Gods Determinations*." Schuldiner 131–50.

Rowe, Karen E. *Saint and Singer: Edward Taylor's Typology and the Poetics of Meditation*. Cambridge: Cambridge UP, 1986.

Scheick, William J. *The Will and the Word: The Poetry of Edward Taylor*. Athens: U of Georgia P, 1974.

Schuldiner, Michael, ed. *The Tayloring Shop: Essays on the Poetry of Edward Taylor in Honor of Thomas M. Davis and Virginia L. Davis*. Newark: U of Delaware P, 1997.

Schweitzer, Ivy. *The Work of Self-Representation: Lyric Poetry in Colonial New England*. Chapel Hill: U of North Carolina P, 1991.

Simpson, Evelyn M., ed. *John Donne's Sermons on the Psalms and Gospels*. Berkeley: U of California P, 1967.

Stanford, Donald E. "*The Poems of Edward Taylor*: The Making of the Yale Edition." *Studies in Puritan American Spirituality* 1 (1990): 3–12.

Taylor, Edward. *Christographia*. Ed. Norman S. Grabo. New Haven: Yale UP, 1962.

———. "Foundation Day Sermon." Davis and Davis, *Edward Taylor's "Church Records" and Related Sermons* 118–58.

———. *The Poems of Edward Taylor*. Ed. Donald E. Stanford. New Haven: Yale UP, 1960.

———. "The Revised Foundation Day Sermon." Davis and Davis, *Edward Taylor's "Church Records" and Related Sermons* 283–373.

———. *Treatise Concerning the Lord's Supper*. Ed. Norman S. Grabo. Lansing: Michigan State UP, 1966.

White, Peter, ed. *Puritan Poets and Poetics: Seventeenth-Century American Poetry in Theory and Practice*. University Park: The Pennsylvania State UP, 1985.

Index

About the Author

ROSEMARY FITHIAN GURUSWAMY is Professor and Chair of English at Radford University. The founding vice president of the Society of Early Americanists, she researches and writes about early Puritan and African American authors. Her essays have appeared in such journals as *Early American Literature* and *New England Quarterly*.